D1549841

SURROUNDED BY HEROES

SURROUNDED BY HEROES

Six Campaigns with Division Headquarters,
82d Airborne Division, 1942–1945

By
LEN LEBENSON

With a Foreword by
Barbara Gavin Fauntleroy

CASEMATE
Philadelphia

Published by
CASEMATE

ISBN 1-932033-58-8

Cataloging-in-publication data is available from the
Library of Congress.

10 9 8 7 6 5 4 3 2 1

CONTENTS

*To all the indomitable troopers of the
82d Airborne Division, 1943–45, who are the
"Heroes" of this memoir.*

FOREWORD
By Barbara Gavin Fauntleroy

I had the pleasure of meeting Len Lebenson and his wife, Alice, in Ireland in 2005. We had flown from New York on the same plane, without knowing each other, then we had three days of sharing a lovely country house hotel and a van, traveling around Northern Ireland. We quickly got to know each other and the other members of our group. We were on a mission to dedicate memorials to the members of the 82nd Airborne Division who had stopped in Ireland in the fall and winter of 1943–44 on their way to England to train and prepare for D-Day.

Len told me that during WWII he had the best job in the Army for an enlisted man because of his skills at typing and drafting. Just two days after reporting to the Induction Center he was loaded onto a train for places unknown and found himself the next day at Ft. Bragg, North Carolina, assigned to the G-3 Section of the 82nd Airborne Division Headquarters. The Division was in need of someone with exactly Len's skills, and he was immediately assigned to the 82nd Headquarters staff. He became one of the few men who served at Headquarters for all six of the Division's campaigns. Rising to the rank of Master Sergeant, he was often selected for special missions because of his intelligence and the trust in which he was held by the Division staff.

He writes about basic training and his first glimpse of the 82nd Airborne Division's commander, General Ridgway on his horse, surveying the new recruits. He describes the officers and men with whom he worked in the Operations Section of the Division Headquarters

before going overseas and during the war. On the troop ship bound for
Africa he met the top ranking NCO of the Army detachment on board
who offered him a shipboard job that he couldn't refuse, which
brought him a green arm band and the run of the ship.

During the invasion of Sicily, Len was selected to go on the ship
with Gen. Ridgway. He discovered that he was also sharing the ship
with Douglas Fairbanks, Jr. and also Generals Weydemeyer and
Patton. While writing about this trip, Len describes "the adventure of
the rope net" a new and hard-won skill. His G-3 group moved back
to Africa, then to Italy as Len managed the responsibility of operations
maps, overlays, orders, after action reports and all of the equipment
needed to produce them.

The next move was again by ship to Ireland for a few months and
then to England, where his G-3 group took part in the normal training activities while also participating in planning for Overlord, the
invasion of France. He was given top-secret "bigoted" status, very rare
for a sergeant, allowing him access to the Division War Room where
plans for Overlord were kept. He retained "bigoted" status for all
later campaigns and thus gained a unique perspective on the plans and
actions of the Division.

On D-Day Len arrived in France by glider. His first mission was to
find the Division Command Post, west of Ste. Mere Eglise, and begin
the routine of updating maps and reports and orders, both incoming
and outgoing. After more than four weeks of battling the Germans in
Normandy, the 82nd was relieved by the 8th Infantry Division and
returned to England. Len created a flow-of-battle map which, along
with text, became the 82nd Airborne's After Action Report for
Normandy.

Back in Leicester, a jump school was set up. Len knew after his
arrival by glider in France that he would prefer going into combat by
any other means. With the departure of Gen. Ridgway and most of his
staff for the newly formed XVIII Airborne Corps, the new Division
Staff, under my Dad as Commanding General, was made up exclu-
sively of paratroopers. The new G-3, Col. Jack Norton, encouraged
Len to go through jump training. He went through a condensed two-
week version of jump school and won his wings in time to make the
daytime jump into Holland. There is a well known photo of my Dad

using one of Len's maps to brief Gen. Sir Miles Dempsey in Holland.

Like most World War II veterans, Len was not immediately ready to examine his experiences and write about them when he returned. It took a while to achieve the perspective and, perhaps, detachment needed to put them down on paper. But after a time, with the affectionate urging of Alice and his family, he wrote his story of World War II. It is a gem. His memory is sharp, and he shares with us the amazing experiences he had and the personalities with whom he served during the war. Len says that he was "surrounded by heroes." He was, without question, a hero himself.

January 17, 1979

Mr. Leonard Lebenson
44 Summit Road
Elizabeth, N. J.   07208

Dear Sgt. Lebenson:

        Thank you for your fine letter of January 2. I remember you very well. Your service to the 82nd was truly outstanding.

        I was particularly interested in your recollection of finding my headquarters. Actually, on the evening of D-Day I put my headquarters in a field about 100 yards from the railroad cut, back toward Ste.-Mere-Eglise. There were no buildings anywhere near there. There were some buildings about 1/2 to 3/4 of a mile away on the edge of the marsh between the railroad and the marsh. That must have been the buildings that you went to. However, I was not there.

Thirty-four years later. Part of a letter from General James Gavin,
one of the author's prized possessions.

INTRODUCTION

Starting in 1945, continuing through 1946 into the following year, literally millions of men (plus a relatively few women who had served) were released from our armed forces back into the uncertainties of civilian life. They included the heroes of Normandy and Iwo Jima, the air battles over Europe and the sea warfare over the vast expanses of the Pacific—and also those who had spent three years on New York's Governors Island, the Presidio in San Francisco, or at Fort Benning, Georgia. Each had his or her own pride in service and legitimacy.

The experiences of the members of my family who served were fairly average. My brother served in the States from 1941 into 1944, finding a niche as a supply sergeant in an infantry company with the 80th Infantry Division—running a payday crap game with his 1st Sergeant that kept them in spending money. He came to the battlefield in September 1944, and was severely wounded and evacuated three weeks later. My half-brother, Herbert, who used the surname "Ross," served in the Coast Guard out of New York.

A step-brother, Wilbur Cutler, had the extreme ill-fortune to be assigned to the outer Air Force defense in Greenland for more than three years, and came out of the mind-deflating boredom of that hellhole a mental wreck from which he never recovered. One brother-in-law, Al Cooper, served with the medics in the Mediterranean and escaped his dead-end only when it was discovered (with a lot of hinting by Al) that he was one of the best ping pong players in the country, and he then traveled around giving exhibitions. Bernie Raved, another brother-in-law, served in the Pacific, came back to the States for OCS, which he did not pass, and ended the war as a corporal. My other two brothers-in-law, both of whom were quite a bit older, also served. Eugene Zimmerman, the older of the two, was discharged early on from the army when age requirements were lowered. The other, Willie, served in a Military Police unit. Of us all, Willie, a good-looking man, looked the best in the photographs that have survived.

I was the one who, through the luck of the draw, participated in many campaigns, as will be seen later on. The profile, however, of the family, was fairly representative. During the war my father proudly displayed a small banner in a living room window with six stars showing the number of servicemen in the family.

When we were so unceremoniously, though happily, dumped back into society, we immediately turned to civilian pursuits far removed from our recent martial activities. For example, I had a son, 19 months old, who I had never seen, a wife and romance to become reacquainted with, and the immediate problem of finding a place to live. In 1942, when I left for the Army, finding an apartment in New York meant spending a day or so in the neighborhood of your choice, locating a place that suited desires and matched resources, and moving in. That system was long gone, as we found out. Housing in late 1945 was already in short supply. By 1946 it was absolutely impossible.

In the midst of this re-immersion into civilian life, talk about the war and individual experiences was remarkably limited. It seemed each veteran had had his own experience and there didn't appear to be much reason to talk about the other guy's. Civilians, even those extremely close, didn't seem to get it (or the teller could not find the proper words to reach the audience). I remember, as my children grew older but still were children, I would from time to time mention something about my war experiences and, even with them, saw the uncomprehending though sympathetic response. Anyway, it was all behind us, and now we were in the present and looking to the future, not on what had happened in the war.

It went on like that for years. I avidly read the various biographies, histories and memoirs as they were published, particularly those that included accounts of the actions I had been engaged in. But it was a relatively private endeavor, shared with my wife, Alice, and nothing I discussed with others.

My experience was the same as that of most veterans. But slowly over the years, some things happened. Doubts, fears, jealousies, feelings of inadequacy, terrible memories, etc., started falling away and it became easier to talk about the war, even though it was still difficult to convey the sense of it to someone who had not been there. We universally scoffed at the versions of war coming from time to time out of Hollywood, and that, too, was hard to explain.

As the years passed, more and more was thought about the past, battlefield visits were made, veteran's organizations joined and supported. For myself, I made a trip back to Normandy in 1970, and Holland and Belgium in later years. I also joined the C-47 Club (named after the WWII transport aircraft) for a D-Day plus 40 trip in 1984 and again for D-Day plus 50 in 1994. I became an active member of the North Jersey Chapter of the 82d Airborne Division Association. I supplied a narrative to Stephen Ambrose for use in the World War II archive he was building, attended a conference of D-Day veterans in New Orleans, and an excerpt from my narrative was included in his best seller, "D-Day."

Because of these growing connections, I was interviewed and given a half-page spread, including photos, in the Bergen (New Jersey) Record's special D-Day plus 50 Anniversary Edition. I also participated in a New Jersey Public Television program on the same anniversary. Later that year I was a speaker at the official New Jersey celebration of the 50th Anniversary of the Battle of the Bulge. So I was getting around quite a bit.

All of this led me to believe I had something to say. I had been in six major campaigns and my service in the G-3 (Operations) Section of the 82d Airborne Division Headquarters afforded a unique position and view. When I was Division Operations Sergeant, I honestly felt I had the best enlisted man's job in the army, and am still of the same opinion. Not too many people, including ex-service personnel, may agree with me. My principal reason is that every order, every action report, every plan, goes through the G-3 section and thus is handled by the Operations Sergeant, who, therefore, was in on the know of all the plans and movements of the Division. At the New Orleans Conference mentioned earlier, I talked with an ex-Master Sergeant of the 101st Division (looking great—he still fit into his uniform) and he disclosed he had been the Intelligence Sergeant of either the 502d or 506th Parachute Regiment. When I told him what my assignment had been, he exclaimed, "Ah, you had the job!"

The passage of time, however, hasn't made it easier for someone who was not in the war to understand what it felt like to be in it. Many years after the event, it seems unthinkable that this otherwise sensible looking man being engaged in conversation may have actually killed someone. I was talking to someone at a meal on an Elderhostel trip and was being questioned about the war and, by the look in her eye, I knew she was formulating how to ask whether I had ever fired at someone and that the next question would get to the inevitable follow up of damage inflicted. I wasn't about to answer her directly if she asked, and diverted the conversation as deftly as I could.

I had occasion to talk with a Congressional Medal of Honor winner at the Battle of the Bulge Commemorative. In order to get this medal one must have "acted above and beyond the call of duty," placed oneself at mortal risk and inflicted serious damage on the enemy. Such actions as throwing oneself on a live grenade, exposing oneself to fire while helping comrades, storming a pill box single handedly, etc., are the types of deeds that lead to consideration for this medal. This hero (for such he was) told me he has been called upon to appear at meetings over the years and to make short speeches but was thinking of giving it up. The reason was that at a recent such event, after a description of his action was given to a class of school kids, a young girl came up to him and rebuked him, asking, "Why did you kill all those people?" He had no answer.

The bane of most soldiers was not knowing what was going on, or what was being planned. This went for the training phase as well as being in combat. Rumors abounded, all having to do with what we did, what we were going to do, who's going to be in charge, when do we get leave, etc., etc. The better "sources"—company clerk, supply personnel, headquarters people, are constantly buttonholed for information—it was called "poop" in those days. And universally, when some bit of poop was gleaned the receivers of the information inevitably then turned on the givers with accusations of, "He's full of it." I personally found this to be true on occasions during the war and, even after, when I told stories of some of my adventures which, as will be seen, had me on occasion close to some very important figures.

Sometime in the mid 1990s, at a Division Association meeting, I was talking with Henry Aust, who was an artillery officer during the war and Gary Szente, who joined the 82d after the war years. Gary, when I mentioned that I held the job that I did asked with a mixture of awe and incredulity in his voice, "How did you ever get that job?"

Aust said, "He obviously earned it."

I appreciated Henry's response. In truth, landing the job had to do with being at the reception center (Camp Upton) at the right time, being presumptively assigned to the G-3 Section even before I arrived at Fort Bragg as the 6th man of a complement of six, joining the group after a brief basic training, seeing the guys who were there before me busted for reasons of breaches of security, the just plain busting of another, the departure of another for OCS, and finally the death of Sergeant Dorant (more about him later), following which I took over the section.

The "Heroes" of this memoir's title are the 12,000 (sometimes greater, sometimes fewer) officers and men of the 82d Airborne Division, which made its indelible mark across the battlefields of the Mediterranean and European Theaters of World War II.

The whole story follows.

HOME - GETTING OUT THAT WHOLE
HISTORY WITH COLOR OPERATION MAPS — ?
AND) SGT ADRIANSON VOLUNTEERING TO GO
ON THE DAYLIGHT RAID DOWN BY THE NIJMEGEN
BRIDGE TO SEIZE A PRISONER — I'M AFRAID
HE WAS WOUNDED OR WORSE — GREAT
TALENT — BIG HEART —

I COULD GO ON — BUT LIKE YOUR
I WANT TO SAY THAT
SUMMARY IN YOUR LETTER — OUR DIV.
WAS VERY FORTUNATE TO HAVE SUCH
A DEDICATED AND) PROFESSIONAL OPN'S
SERGEANT. — YOU COULD FOLLOW THE BATTLE,
HANDLE CRITICAL MESSAGES, RADIO TRAFFIC
TYPE LIKE A MACHINE GUN, COMPOSE AND)
PRODUCE OVERLAYS (WITH THOSE SLIMEY
JELLY PADS!) KEEP OUR DECISION -MAKING
OPERATIONS MAPS, AND) STILL FIND TIME
TO HELP OTHERS — AND SHAVE -AND) LAUGH—
YOU WERE MY RIGHT ARM — AND I'LL
ALWAYS BE GRATEFUL —
LETS STAY IN TOUCH — FAITHFULLY,
Jack Norton

THE PAPERS SOFTEN — DID GET TO ME - BUT ERA MISSING : NOW H HAVE YOUR ADDRESS!

Forty-two years later. Extract from a letter from Lt. General Jack Norton
(82d Airborne Division G-3 during WWII), which reads, in part:
"Our Div. was very fortunate to have such a dedicated and professional
Opn's Sergeant. You could follow the battle, handle critical messages,
radio traffic, type like a machine gun, compose and produce overlays
(with those slimey jelly pads!) keep our decision-making operations
maps, and still find time to help others—and shave, and laugh—
you were my right arm, and I'll always be grateful."

1

ARMY INDUCTION

To the beginning:

I was drafted in September of 1942. In those days the procedure was to take the Army (or other branch) physical and not be sworn in until passing it and being accepted for duty. Then the individual had two weeks to go home and clear up his affairs before reporting for duty. This system was used to avoid someone quitting a job, for example, before taking the physical and then being left high and dry if he failed.

The physical was taken at Governors Island in New York Harbor. When I had received my notice for induction to the Army I made a hurry-up visit to Coast Guard Headquarters to see whether I could volunteer for that branch, but was turned down because of not meeting the minimum height requirement. So, with hundreds of others that day at Governors Island, I went through a battery of physical and psychological tests and was given a clean bill of health on all accounts.

Speculation was that if you told the psychological tester that you were homosexual you would be immediately rejected for induction. One of the men in my group traveling to Governors Island was very flamboyant in his sexual orientation, told the examiner that he was homosexual and, indeed, was rejected for service. In those days, none of us knew too much about all that and treated the whole idea (out of ignorance) with amusement.

So after being accepted physically, I had the two-week grace period before reporting for duty. A lot had to be done, including giving up our love-nest one bedroom apartment on East 36th Street (which we would regret three years down the road). For various reasons, including job, family and other considerations, we had been living in unmarried state while telling everyone we were married—Alice had been wearing her hastily purchased $3.50 ring from Saks on 34th Street. Our number one priority for this period was to get married before I entered the Army. There was no traditional wedding. Instead we went to the City Clerk in City Hall, found out we needed two witnesses, frantically recruited two unknowns from the street, and got married. Then we prepared for the wrench of separation as best we could.

I reported as directed to Penn Station and joined a large group coming in at the same time for a trip on the Long Island Railroad to Camp Upton in Yaphank. When we arrived, I had my first exposure to the Army rumor syndrome, as we all tried to gather some idea of what was about to happen to us. I found out from the "old hands" that the testing to be done, the issuance of uniforms, etc., and the medical processing would take two to three days, after which, in a short time, the individual would receive an assignment, usually as part of a large group, and would leave Upton on a troop train under sealed orders. So it looked like we would be there anywhere from four days to a week. There were a few pay phones on the base, with long lines at them, and after waiting for my turn I failed to make connection with Alice the first day, but fortunately was able to do so the second.

Now I was a soldier, joining the thousands of equally unprepared men who were being sworn in every day. The un-reality of it all was difficult to take seriously. But, on to the next steps: Part of the procedure included filling out a job history, listing civilian skills, as the attempt was to find the square peg for the square hole.

When I graduated High School in 1933 in the depths of the Depression (the banks were closed shortly afterward when Roosevelt took office in March of that year), there were few, if any, jobs. About a day or so after graduation a guy who I knew not too well—all I remember now is that his name was Nat—called at my house and asked if I was looking for a job! Nat was still in High School and had a job after school working in a candy/ice cream store the next block over from where I lived. It seemed that in the adjoining store there was a struggling one-man real estate office owned and operated by an Al Roberts who wanted someone to man the office while he wasn't there, which was most of the time. I jumped at the opportunity and got the job for the princely sum of $5 per week! Not only that, but within a couple of weeks I had secured jobs (better than mine) for two other recent graduates in the same block of stores. Roy Schwartz went to work in a small advertising agency and the other guy, whose name escapes me, in a drug store.

But I had very little to do in this office which consisted physically of two desks and a number of chairs in a small space about 15 feet square. Part of the equipment was an old Oliver typewriter and, as I discovered, an instruction book for touch typing. With so little to do in the office, I decided to learn to type, spending an hour or two per day on the machine. After a few months, and before I left the office I was a fairly proficient typist.

But another opportunity struck and I left for a better paying job ($10 per week) in the garment center in Manhattan. (At the time we were living in Queens). My older brother, Milton, had been working for a textile firm as a shipping clerk/delivery boy and the firm, Reliable Textile Co., at 200 West 37th St., needed another body so I was brought in. This was in 1933 and I worked in the Garment Center until 1941.

By this time the war clouds were gathering over our country and there was a great expansion of work relating to armaments. A friend of mine, Burt Garrett, was conducting an evening class for the Federation of Architects, Engineers, Chemists and Technicians. At his urging, and our recognition that this was the proper thing to do, I enrolled in his class and after a few months had enough rudimentary skills so that I was able to quit the Garment Center and went to work for a die maker as a draftsman, and later for an electrical equipment manufacturer. My combined time on those jobs was slightly over a year.

When it came time to list civilian skills on the forms at Camp Upton I checked off both typist and draftsman. Little did I know that these were two of the skills the army was really looking for! The standing joke at the time was about the First Sergeant lining up his men and asking for a show of hands of who could drive a truck, and handing all of those foolish enough to reply brooms with orders to start sweeping.

I recall the guy reviewing my form looking at me skeptically and asking, "You're a draftsman and can also type?" He shrugged when I answered "Yes."

We had arrived at Camp Upton in the afternoon, were assigned to our barracks, and spent the rest of the day drawing uniforms and other equipment. The next day we were awakened early. There was a roll call and some of the men who had been there for some days were notified they were leaving and to get all their stuff together. Those who had come in when I did proceeded to a battery of tests and interviews which lasted most of the day. The next morning we had a roll call again and, to my amazement, my name was on the list of those who were to leave that day!

So there I was, two days after reporting for duty, along with what turned out to be about six hundred others, looking, I'm sure, laughable in our new uniforms self-consciously worn, dragging our two barracks bags along behind us. We straggled down a long street until reaching a railroad staging area and loaded onto the train for the journey which had us arriving in what we made out to be the Washington DC station about nightfall. I took advantage of the stop to slip a postcard I had written home to a railroad worker who passed through the car. It turned out he mailed it for me, the first time I took advantage of the free postal service privilege offered servicemen.

Speculation was rife as to where we were going, but being in the Washington depot kind of indicated we were headed for the south. There were a couple of occasions on the trip when roll calls were taken and it seemed as if I were part of a small group of about twelve who were listed together among the larger group. For the most part we were anxious and mystified, getting to know each other while digesting the obvious – we were in the Army now.

The train chugged on into the night. I had no sleep and at a time near morning the train stopped for some hours. With daybreak there was a stirring, we were given breakfast in the mess car, and we noted that we were parked in a wooded area. Then some athletic looking officers boarded the train seeming to take control of the situation. To our astonishment they were wearing Divisional (as we later found out) insignia with two A's in a square with a curved strip above it with the word "Airborne." So what were we doing there? We knew there were parachute troops in the army but also knew they were all volunteers. While we were buzzing about this turn of events, the train lurched forward, proceeding a short distance to a cleared embankment, and there, pulled up in a square formation, was an army band that started belting out a lively military tune. For us? What a contrast! This very professional band was playing stirring marches and we were 600 very, very confused amateurs.

Anyway, it certainly got our blood moving. We also noticed a row of army trucks waiting for us manned by lithe soldiers all wearing parachute insignias on their caps, obviously amused at the sight we were providing. We were hustled onto the trucks along with our belongings and motored in a very dusty convoy to an outdoor amphitheater on what we soon found out was Fort Bragg, North Carolina, the home of the newly formed 82d and 101st Airborne Divisions.

When we were finally seated, our attention was drawn to the stage on which were assembled a number of officers looking resplendent in brown leather jackets. Someone took the microphone and advised us that we were (the truth was out!) now part of the 82d Airborne Division. He said he was pleased to introduce us to the "finest division commander in the United States Army," and then, from the wings, purposefully bounded (I use the word advisedly) Major General Matthew Ridgway. Ridgway gave a short welcoming speech, and advised us that we were to be given an intense basic training after which we would join our regular units. He was impressive, and, as I found out later, he was for real.

Then we were told to assemble in groups as our names were called and (this day was really full of surprises) my name was among the first called and I noticed that our group of twelve was together. We loaded our barracks bags onto a truck and a Sergeant took charge of us and marched us a few hundred yards to a nearby barracks, all the while keeping up a pleasant line of banter. His name was Tulio Malagrida and was an agreeable surprise for those of us who expected someone to bark at us. He informed us right away that we were to be with Headquarters Company of the Division, and we were quartered on one floor of the barracks, the rest of the floor and the upper floor occupied, as we found out later, by men who were assigned to Division Headquarters.

We always remembered our first encounter with the 82d being Tulio and he remembered it as well as he remained contented, it seemed, as a three-stripe sergeant for the duration of the war. We had a special bond.

The final point to be made is that I was selected for the 82d Airborne on my second day in the Army. A request had been made by the 82d for 600 men, most of whom ended up in the 326th Glider Infantry. The request had been routed to Camp Upton. Included in the request was the need by the Division G-3 for a draftsman, preferably one who could type. The paperwork reached Upton just as I was coming through there and the process was such that, if I had come there a few days later or earlier, I would have had a completely different Army career.

That was the beginning of how I came to hold what I considered the best assignment for an enlisted man in the entire U.S. Army— Operations Sergeant of the 82d Airborne Division. In the end I became one of those lithe, trim, soldierly looking men, eventually had both glider and parachute training, and had some interesting and, at times, harrowing experiences along the way.

2

BASIC TRAINING

And then there was basic training.

In retrospect, it could have better prepared us for the rigors and skills of being a soldier, but we didn't know too much about the whole affair, so at the time it seemed a good and proper deal.

It lasted eight weeks and included learning the courtesies of the service and the meaning of the pertinent Articles of War (mostly how and when to salute and the penalties for not obeying orders). We didn't at that time know the nuances of what was a "direct order" and what was not.

Also we did close-order drill, manual of arms, marching in small and large formations, and received instruction in the care and cleaning of the M-1 rifle. The latter meant that we spent an inordinate amount of time pushing oiled rags through the bores of our rifles and also learned how to assemble and disassemble said rifle blindfolded. To our amazement, we all learned.

We did the obligatory washing down of the wooden barracks floor using toothbrushes, and suffered through white glove inspections where the object was for the inspecting officer to run his gloved hand over any surface in the barracks without it being stained by dirt.

We marched each morning to the parade ground or the post theater, wherever the schedule demanded, in a column of twos (called a "column of ducks") and after a while Sergeant Fleming had us whistling tunes like "The Caissons go Rolling Along" as we marched. At first we were self conscious about it, but after we got over that, the music buoyed our spirits and lightened our steps, particularly on the

way "home" after the day's activities. The signal for the whistling was
J. D. Phillips calling out, "How about a little ditty?" and off we would
go.

We practiced aiming our rifles through the process called triangu-
lation, and one of the high points of the training was our visit to the
rifle range. There we all took our turns operating and marking targets
for the other guys and had our own turns at 200 and 300 yards, using
the four firing positions we had learned: standing, prone, kneeling and
sitting.

As usual, scuttlebutt was part of the experience. Rumor had it that
those of us who did well would automatically be transferred to rifle
companies and the failures assigned to the medics and headquarters.
In the event, I know of no one who didn't do his best; most of us were
rated as Marksman and a few made Expert and Sharpshooter.

We also had the back-breakers—bayonet practice and hand-to-
hand combat. Bayonet practice was the kind of thing that one referred
to when sneering at how ridiculous Army training was. Most of the
drill (particularly the positions where the drill sergeants wanted to
instill pain) had one standing in an awkward extended position with
the rifle pointed straight toward the "enemy" with the bayonet fixed
in place. The command "Hold!" made one stay in that position for
endless seconds while everything was checked for accuracy of execution. The strain on the arm and back was huge. This drill was for the
bigger, stronger guys, of which I was not one.

Similarly with hand-to-hand combat. This was done usually after
viewing a training film where judo and knife fighting professionals
showed "how it is done." We were shown techniques for throat-slit-
ting, arm-breaking and other goodies. And then we would try these
things on each other. One's opponent usually was the man who happened to be in the opposite rank when the orders were given; in many
cases it pitted the biggest guys against the smallest (at least it always
seemed that way). The non-coms in charge were on the lookout for
malingerers (which meant all of us) and insisted on seeing genuine
effort. I took many a friendly beating.

We also spent a lot of time in the Post Theater where we were
shown the Army Training Films and also had lectures on various
aspects of the work we were doing. We were a group of about 600, the

vast majority of whom were assigned to the 326th Glider Infantry and a relatively few, about 30 in all, assigned among Division Headquarters, the 307th Airborne Medical Company and the 307th Airborne Signal Company. The 30 of us were organized into one platoon with officers furnished by the 326th. The 12 of us destined for Division Headquarters Company were assigned a Sergeant, Fleming by name, and Private First Class, J. D. Phillips. Sgt. Fleming was a find, and I'm sure he went on to bigger and better things. When our training was over, he shipped out to Officers Candidate School and he had the makings of a fine officer. He was from Kentucky, moderate in size, extremely well built and good looking, and had all the skills to shepherd a group such as we were through the first anxious weeks in the Army.

Phillips was from Oklahoma, spoke with a southwestern drawl and also handled his business well. He was a skilled infantryman and knew his weapons. As the war progressed, the functions of the Division Reconnaissance Platoon expanded and J. D. wound up there, going through the war carrying the rank of PFC. He deserved better.

During training we also took one long hike with the expected result of blisters and fatigue. On the whole we did the brief training quite well in that we did what was asked of us. We had one interesting experience early on. It was the first Sunday we were in camp and, since we were confined to camp for the duration of basic training (no passes), Fleming had us out doing close-order drill, which meant marching up and down in single file. Our favorite order was "to the rear, march!" which had us practically running into each other as we strained to keep from collapsing in laughter. Suddenly we noticed we were being observed by a horseman on a splendid black mount—and it turned out to be General Ridgway! We suppressed our laughing as best we could and continued following Fleming's orders until he drew us up in a rank in front of the General. Fleming barked, "Halt! "Right face!" and then saluted the General. We were standing there hardly daring to draw breaths, and the General commended us on our military bearing after only a few days in the service. Then he drew Fleming aside and spoke to him briefly. He later told us the General had complimented him on how we looked and that he reminded Fleming he should have immediately reported to Ridgway when he was noticed rather than waiting until we were stopped in front of him. We all thought that was a little chickenshit but Fleming was on cloud nine. As I later found out about Ridgway, he never (!) forgot a name and I'm sure that little incident gave Fleming's career a boost.

The overall command of our training platoon shifted around among a number of officers from the 326th and also a couple of non-coms, one of whom was a typical backwoods sergeant from South Carolina, delighted to be able to lord it over us Yankees. His favorite expression was "You guys remind me of a bunch of monkeys fucking a football." Anyway, we all survived. It didn't take much to make us laugh, probably because, deep down, the whole idea of us becoming soldiers was somewhat hilarious.

We would have these little discussion sessions, after a movie or lecture, where we would try to apply some knowledge we had just picked up. One day, after a session on field sanitation in which it was demonstrated how to dig a slit trench (for use as a latrine) the word "feces" was used a few times—probably the first time most of us had heard that word. Later, when we were together for follow-up discussion in our small group, Fisher, our perennial goof-off, raised his hand and started a serious question in his bumbling way with "Suppose I have to take a feces . . .", and couldn't get any further because we all broke up. For the better part of the next three years, whenever any of us were together and needed a laugh, someone would start in with "Suppose I have . . ." It worked every time, which will give you an idea of Army humor.

The destination of my group of twelve was, as we found out later, determined even before we arrived at Fort Bragg. Mason and Brown were going to G-1 (Personnel), Schneider was going to G-2 (Intelligence), I was going to G-3 (Operations), Dzubak to G-4 (Logistics), Snow to the Division Surgeon, Dziuban to the Division Chemical Warfare Office, Marotta to the Division Inspector General, and Minerick, Jones, Fisher and Ricker to the Adjutant General's Office.

We were all going in as low men on the totem pole in the various staff sections because we were the finish in the fleshing out of Division Headquarters. And as is the way in the Army, these assignments were almost immediately altered. Schneider shattered his arm on an obstacle course not too long after we ended training, and Fisher was transferred somewhere quite quickly, so our group was reduced from twelve to ten. Marotta later felt he was in a dead end in the IG office so asked, and was given, a transfer to the Reconnaissance Platoon. The rest of us stayed in the slots as listed above. Mason rose the highest, receiving a commission to Lieutenant.

The basic training lasted more or less eight weeks, I don't recall exactly. In those days the Army was expanding rapidly. The 82d Infantry Division had been activated only about two months when Ridgway took over from Omar Bradley, and at the same time, the two airborne divisions were created out of the one infantry division. At the time of the initial organization about only one third of the division was made up of parachutists, the parachute infantry regiment assigned to the 82d being the 504th. Later, in January 1943, a 2nd parachute regiment—the 505th—was added, and then the division became two-thirds parachute (volunteers) and one-third glider (non-volunteers). The headquarters of the division and most of the special troops were glider. Two thirds of the engineers and the artillery were parachute after the early 1943 reorganization.

The 326th Glider Infantry, which received most of the men with whom I had traveled from Camp Upton, was detached from the Division when the 505th was attached, and made its way to Alliance, Nebraska, where it became part of the 13th Airborne Division. When that happened, only thirty of the six hundred or so who went from Upton to Bragg in the Fall of 1942 remained with the Division. So that rounds out our basic training. In retrospect it seems that a lot of us were shortchanged in our training because of the speed with which our army was expanding. It should be observed that all the individuals mentioned above with whom I was in contact generally gave a good account of themselves throughout the war.

Our last day's drill ended on a high note. It is customary at the end of the day's activities for the troops (in our case 12 guys) to be brought to attention on the company street in a rank facing the drill sergeant, and the Inspection Arms routine is observed. This is how it worked: The men are drawn up in ranks, at attention, with arms at "port," in which position the rifle is held diagonally across the chest. The order, "Inspection" is given at which time the men in ranks slide back the lever over the bullet chamber into its locked position, and then look quickly down into the chamber to see that the chamber is empty. One's head is then returned to normal position, and then the other half of the order, "Arms," is given. At that point the men thrust a finger into the rifle chamber, release the lock, the lever closes and then the trigger is pulled and the firing mechanism goes off with a loud snap. The whole idea is to do this in sync and we never got it right. There were two tell-tale clicks—one when the lever was slid open, the other when it was closed, and then there was also the sound of the firing mechanism.

But on this last day, which we knew ended our training, we got it right and the successive sounds of the levers opening, then closing, followed by the snap of the firing mechanism, came from we twelve as if we were one, and, believe it or not, we were happy and proud about it.

3

THE ROOKIES

What are the odds that in a group of 12, such as we recruits were, there would be one guy named Dzubak and one named Dziuban? Both were from Westchester County and both were of Polish extraction, but the similarity ended there.

Steve Dzubak was the youngest of our little group, and the most reticent at the beginning, but he blossomed out as time wore on and became a productive member of the G-4 (Supply and Transportation) section. He had a shy smile, an engaging manner and became very well liked. Because of the confusion with the names and also the misguided humor of the others, he was called "douche-bag," a name that stuck. He didn't mind. He pronounced his name as if there wasn't any letter "d," in other words as "Zubak."

Joe Dziuban was one of the older guys—he may have been in his late thirties. He was short, stocky and balding. He had the ill-luck to be stuck in the Chemical Warfare office for the duration under the leadership of Colonel Geiger (otherwise known as "Colonel Phosgene") and also Sergeant McCormick who wore the eyeglasses with very small lenses which were issued for use with a gas mask. (It made him look like the beady-eyed guy in the horror movie who applies the torture.)

Joe was very gregarious and a favorite of all. He pronounced his name as "Juban," leading to all sorts of complications. From time to time we would have these assemblages for having the Articles of War re-read to us, or perhaps a medical exam (usually for venereal disease) and we would be banded together with the Headquarters Company guys, making a group of several hundred with someone calling the roll who knew none of us.

The same thing would happen all the time. When his tongue-twister name came in front of the roll caller, Joe would invariably pipe up, "Forget the D, pronounce it like a J, Juban." The officer reading the roll would then say something like, "Oh, do I have it wrong, are you with the J's?" Joe would then reply, "No, you are in the right place, but it is pronounced Juban." This would go back and forth for some time while we were all rolling over the floor (figuratively) and the roll-caller became somewhat irritated and then it would subside and become smoothed out. This was solved for us when we decided to call him "Dizban" which stuck for the duration.

So Dzubak and Dziuban became "Douche-bag" and "Dizban."

Another of our little group was Bernie Brown. Brownie was a minor league theatrical producer who had many years experience on the fringes of the Broadway scene. He was also in his thirties. Theater was his life and he was fortunate in winding up attached to the G-1 section which had responsibility for personnel, morale and entertainment falling under their aegis. Brownie saw the contradictions in the city boy becoming soldier and was the first to break down into laughter when we were doing close-order drill, dragging the rest of us with him. He stayed in the same post during the war, which became more important when we got to Great Britain and later. He was responsible for putting together a pretty good musical entertainment, using English ATS girls, during our stay in Leicester. The guy who wrote the music for that show, Carl Sigman, had joined us there. Later Carl became a very successful composer of popular music, authoring at least one successful Broadway show, "Make Mine Manhattan."

Just before going overseas, Brownie married a very gorgeous showgirl who then became a member of the cast of a long running Broadway musical, "Rosalinda." When we first arrived overseas, he received a steady stream of letters from her. After a while they started being less frequent and he confided in me that he didn't think she would remain steady considering all the temptations she was facing.

Sure enough, it wasn't long before he received a "Dear John" letter which he took very calmly. He told me with a "what the hell" that he had been happy in the brief but glorious fling he'd had with her.

One memory about Brownie sticks in mind: We had our introduction to dysentery in Africa when the flies that hovered most of the day around the open latrines would make bee lines to us while we were eating our chow in the open from our mess kits, eating with one hand and fruitlessly waving the flies away with the other. It didn't work too well and most of us were down with the "G-I's" at one time or other. We actually didn't fully get rid of it until many months later when we boarded Navy vessels (clean, clean) for the trip to Ireland. I was standing talking with Brownie one day after breakfast when his eyes clouded over. He clenched his teeth and said, "I can't hold it in," and actually had his bowels erupt as we talked. Poor guy! It was something even I (the great needler) never mentioned to him later.

As a further aside having to do with infections: I developed a couple of open sores on a finger while in Africa that persisted until I reported to the sick bay on that same Navy transport. I was treated with some powder and, after a few days, the sores disappeared.

Perhaps our most interesting guy was Charlie Mason, also from Westchester County. No one ever found out anything about his background. Mason was older, obviously well educated, and was noticeable mainly because of the carefully waxed moustache that he fastidiously groomed. He received no mail from home, hung out with no one, smoked but did not drink or go out. He spent most of his spare time in the G-l office to which he was assigned. He was tall and thin, somewhat ungainly with a walk that can best be described as modified Groucho Marx—leaning forward. Charlie was approachable only by either Ricker or me among the group of twelve and seemed to like it that way. He was a student of the war and read newspapers and magazines assiduously. He also did very well in assignments such as taking care of his equipment, assembly of weapons and the like. He was determined to make a go of it.

In so doing he took dead aim at Master Sergeant Colter, his chief in G-l. Charlie cozied up to Colonel Schellhanmer, the head of the section, and after months of relentless flattery and brown-nosing, it worked. Colter was gone and Mason was eventually promoted to his place. Most everybody resented Mason for this, accusing him of undermining Colter by continually sucking up to Schellhammer. All true. But in later times I found I could always get the information I needed from Mason.

Vinnie Ricker, also from Westchester, was one of our youngest guys, probably about 20, and he had worked briefly for the New York Central Railroad before entering the service. Rick was 6'4" and gangly, very uncoordinated at the beginning while we were being whipped into shape with calisthenics and close-order drill. He handled everything well and was obviously a man of strong character. The Adjutant General's Office, to which he was assigned, was the largest of the staff sections with over 20 men, being responsible for all the records of the Division. Sgt. Lawlor, who was the top enlisted man in the group, became ill and was replaced by Sgt. Kaplan, and then later Vin was promoted to the spot vacated by Kaplan, leapfrogging a whole bunch of guys. He also was a good friend.

The rest of the group who stayed with us were Jones, Snow, Minerick and Marotta. As mentioned earlier, Marotta was assigned to the Inspector General's Office, which was inactive for many months because of the illness of Colonel Barrett, and he itched to become more active. He finally sought and was given a transfer to the Reconnaissance Platoon, which after we reached Holland became a very important part of the Division. Marotta never regretted the transfer.

Roly-poly Jonesy came from Utica, New York, was as good-natured as they come, and was beloved by all. He didn't have a mean bone in his body. Snow came from New York and would have been everybody's choice to succeed because of his attitude, appearance and intelligence. Unfortunately for him he was assigned to the Division Surgeon who had two enlisted men in the section, one of whom was "hash-mark" Harris, a regular army holdover who was his chief. Snow never forced an opportunity to leave that dead-end and possibly regrets it to this day.

Last but not least of our group was Bill Minerick, who also hailed from Westchester. He was the humorous life of the basic training period, was assigned to the Adjutant General, and along with Ricker and Jones figuratively disappeared among the filing cabinets.

They were a good group.

4

FORT BRAGG

Our brief basic training was over. For better or worse, we were now ready to join the team and take on our assignments, whatever they turned out to be.

Washed and polished, in a clean uniform, I reported to G-3 as directed. I had no idea what G-3 meant, but soon found out it was the plans and training section of the General's staff. Heady stuff. I had made my way over to the white frame building near the post theater complex and reported, using the newly learned salute and verbal protocols. Lt. Colonel Boyd was pleasant enough and I was turned over to Master Sergeant Chester Dorant, who was the chief of the enlisted men of the group. Chester took me under his wing, showed me the ropes, and was a friend from day one. More detail on that later.

Other things were happening as well. Finishing the training made passes and a short furlough available to us. During training, Alice had visited Ft. Bragg and managed to get a room somewhere in Fayetteville, and First Sergeant Collins looked the other way while he ostentatiously put a pass to town on his desk within my reach while telling me no one in my group was allowed off the post. Illustrating that there was more than one way to honor orders. I was forever grateful to him. Anyway, we spent a hectic, brief overnight in Fayetteville and it was a marvelous break from the routine of the prior weeks.

We had toyed with the idea of Alice following me to Fayetteville, getting a job and a place to live, so that I could visit evenings and over the weekends. We vetoed the idea because it was obvious that I wasn't going to be around for too long and there were other considerations—the conditions in Fayetteville itself, getting a new job, etc., and also the need for everyone to pitch into the war effort. Alice could obviously do much more in her job in New York than slinging hash in a Southern town.

Later, in December, I had a furlough home. I had just been promoted to T/5 (equivalent to Corporal), and proudly wore my new rank on my uniform. Alice had rented an apartment for a week in Sunnyside and we spent a too-brief time there before I had to return.

We developed a routine of meeting every few weeks for an overnight stay in Richmond, Virginia (halfway between Fayetteville and New York). We stayed at the William Byrd Hotel which was across the street from the railroad station, had one good meal in the evening, breakfast in bed, and then back to our respective homes (if one could call the barracks home). Just before I went overseas, I got a counterfeit three-day pass and came up to New York. We had a room in a hotel on 23rd St. near Lexington Avenue. I knew at the time that we were shortly to ship out and can't remember whether I passed on the classified news to Alice. Anyway it was the last weekend we spent together for almost two and a half years, and during it our firstborn son, Joe, was conceived.

Back in the Army—during the five-month period from the end of basic training until we left Fort Bragg—I was the sixth man in a six-man department. I was promoted to T/4 (equivalent to Sergeant) a month after being elevated to T/5, not realizing that I would hold this rank until after the Normandy campaign. My intention was to apply to Officer Candidate's School as soon as the opportunity arose, but that didn't happen until we had arrived in Ireland at the end of 1943.

Finding myself in a larger group than our original twelve recruits, I was now part of the combined Headquarters and Headquarters Company, about 200 men, and had a whole new bunch of names to learn. We had two Baldwins, one named H.C., one Fitts and one Fritz, Fitts' name being A.C., so we had additional confusion of who was HC and who was AC. Fritz' name was E.V., named as we found out for the Socialist Labor Leader and presidential candidate of the 20's, Eugene V. Debs. Fritz, who later joined us at G-3 when Information & Education came under us, was a hell of a nice guy from Ohio, the sixth child with five older sisters, and it looked like he needed being taken care of. We called him, affectionately, E. Victim.

There was a Sergeant, Ben E. Wright, who was in charge of food inspection and wore a medical insignia with a "V" on it (for Veterinarian). In civilian life he was a mortician, which, as would be suspected, was always good for a laugh given the sporadic quality of our food.

Then there were Unocic and Constantine, two Privates who were happy at being at the low end of the totem pole. They took care of the furnaces, mopped up the latrines and did other crap jobs, but they always did it with flair. When they moved from one location to another, they would carry their brooms or shovels on their shoulder as they would a rifle and march in step, seemingly enjoying the whole procedure. They did this through the duration whenever we were in a stable camp.

Headquarters Co. was initially presided over by First Sgt. Collins (he of my first pass to town). He was soon followed by Hubert Langley, a handsome Georgian known for his winning smile (belying the stereotype of his position). Lang, as he was called, remained with us until the end of the war.

More importantly, I now was in contact with the men with whom I would serve in the days ahead. Of the group, none was more important in these initial stages than Sgt. Dorant. Chester came from Cleveland and was Regular Army, which meant he was not a draftee. He had been in the 9th Infantry Division and, like many "Old Army" guys, was expert in Army Regulations and knew all the ins and outs of garrison life. He was a couple of years older than the rest of us and, as I found out to be common, considered himself to be very much the ladies man.

He was quite a complex guy. Like many of us, he was a child of the Depression and found his way to a job by joining the peacetime Army, which in the late 30's was very much looked down upon. The explosion in the size of the armed forces begun in 1940 afforded advancement for all those like him who were already in the Army, knew the rules and regulations, and who could be used as the nuclei for the enormous number of units being formed. Those among them who had something on the ball became the First Sergeants, Warrant Officers and Officer Candidates of the new Army.

And Chester found himself assigned as the Chief NCO of the G-3 Section of one of the new Airborne Divisions. Although he had none of the skills (couldn't type, draw, make an overlay, assemble a map from sections, keep a journal, etc.) he had the guys under him who could do those things. As an administrator, assigning the work fairly, keeping everybody happy, dealing with the officers and all the rest, he was superb, bringing an acute consciousness of the status of enlisted men to his job. For example, when I joined G-3, directly from Camp Upton and the brief basic training in Ft. Bragg, there were five men in the Section. The Table of Organization called for six and that last man was to have the rank of Technician Grade 4 (T/4), which was the pay rank equivalent to Sergeant. As soon as I had completed one month in G-3 (the earliest possible date), Chester had the necessary paperwork drawn up for my promotion to T/5 (two stripes) and placed it on the colonel's desk for signature, and a month later did the same thing with the papers for promotion to T/4—again at the earliest possible date.

We were a happy group in G-3, actually the envy of the other Headquarters sections. Durant was responsible for much of the harmony, achieved with the knowledge and consent of Colonel Boyd and his officers. The others in our group included Harold Wilhelm from Richmond Hill, NY, who was a Staff Sergeant, Sergeant Bob Witty from Ohio, and T/4's Bill Mehrholz from Chicago and Graddy Richard from Louisville.

Fort Bragg covers about 40 miles east to west. The post is on the eastern end, there are extensive firing ranges in the middle and, on the western end was the town of Southern Pines. Witty had a car on the post and most weekends Dorant, Witty and Richard would head out to Southern Pines for "honky-tonking." Wilhelm's wife had followed him to Fayetteville and taken a small apartment while she waitressed days, and Wilhelm spent most weekends and many other nights with her. Mehrholz stayed on the post.

But back to what I did for "a living." An Infantry Division is organized into squads, platoons, companies, battalions and regiments, with equivalent formations for the artillery and other ancillary units. Training schedules were published every day for all these groups, which meant we collected, collated and published data from all the units in the command. We also provided the overall proposed schedules. Generally, training followed a cycle of platoon-size problems, followed by company, then battalion, then regimental exercises, always followed by a division-size exercise. The cycle would run over a number of months and then would be repeated—not exactly, but in general outline.

We at G-3 produced the plans, schedules and maps for the exercises, and kept records of all the operational activities of the Division. The usual map-making activity consisted of producing overlays—transparent sheets that carried data registered with printed maps that could be overlaid over the pertinent maps and read accordingly. The method of printing these overlays was by hectograph, which consisted of developing a master (using special pencils, pens or carbon type paper), transferring the master onto a jellied sheet, using water for the purpose, and then making copies from the jellied sheet by placing an individual sheet of paper on the jellied sheet, applying some pressure to it, and then pulling it off. It was, as can be seen, a slow process, but it is the one we used throughout the war, becoming quite skilled at it as time wore on. Register marks were placed on the overlay so that it could be placed over the map being used and read successfully.

We also handled training aids, and made plans for the occasional Division Review and/or special event. We kept quite busy. Even though the Table of Organization (T/O) called for six men, we received three more in January. Most of the Headquarters sections also received some additional men. The reason for this was to prepare for possible attrition, which, as it turned out, our G-3 group experienced.

But soldiering, in the form of falling out for drill or taking part in hiking and field exercises, was over as soon as our initial basic training was finished. We got up with Reveille, had breakfast, went to the Headquarters building, leaving only for lunch and evening meal at the mess hall, and then were off until the next day. Since the routine was standardized with very few exceptions, we were able to plan among each other, with the agreement of Sgt. Dorant, to run private errands or take a morning off for various reasons. Weekends were mostly free.

As soon as I got my third stripe, there was no more KP or other such detail. It was a matter of pride with us that we were able to avoid, although we were supposed to participate in, various things such as parades, reviews and the like. Stretching the limits of our structured schedule, we could also go over to the main recreation building which had the Service Club, a large lounge area, a restaurant and a library. We were able to "send out for coffee," or to spend an hour or so over there shooting the breeze. Best of all, I was able to sneak out from the post for unauthorized overnight trips, of which I took several to Richmond with faked "pass" in hand. These were the benefits of being in HQ.

There was one exercise we had to participate in—that was a so-called Command Post Exercise (CPX) which was designed precisely for the operational headquarters units, the G's 1, 2, 3 and 4, and the corresponding regimental and battalion staffs. A scenario would be developed which would test our ability to send and receive messages, orders, and the ancillary functions of keeping a journal of the events and a properly posted map. That was our one field experience before going overseas.

We also had demonstrations of new weapons, such as bazookas and rifle grenades, which were developed for the infantryman as anti-tank weapons. Another demonstration was of the gliders we were to use. This was done at Pope Field, in front of an audience that included Anthony Eden, Foreign Secretary of England.

Then we went off to Maxton, North Carolina, for a week of acclimatization to these gliders, called the CG4A. Instructions were given in how to load equipment onto them, how to enter and leave the door, etc. The week was climaxed by taking a ride in the glider. None of us were impressed with them—they were made of metal tubing, plywood and canvas with the wires of the controls exposed throughout the cabin. I managed to avoid the glider ride because there weren't enough of them to carry everyone, and some of us rode in the tow planes, the famous C-47's, called the Dakota by the English and the DC-3 by the Douglas Company which designed and produced them. It was my first airplane ride.

It can be seen that we in Headquarters went overseas into combat zones with a very limited amount of training in infantry essentials. We had little weapons experience. I, for example, never saw an infantry mortar until I ran across one in Italy. We never got to work with or fire a machine gun. We didn't throw a grenade. Artillery was a foreign country. The air training which we, who were slated to use gliders, received was fragmentary at best. Up until loading for the actual invasion of Normandy in a glider, I'd had exactly one such training experience. That was in England, either in March or April of 1944.

We did have gas mask drill as part of basic training, which concluded by removing them in a shed full of tear gas, having to stand there for about thirty seconds with our gas masks removed before being permitted, coughing and retching, to leave the shed.

The hurry-up training we experienced was repeated throughout the armed forces as we jumped from 100,000 men in the late 30's to a total of 14,000,000 men (and women) in arms. The leaders had to be developed, almost from scratch, and the miracle is that we did it so well.

One of the details we did have to pull as part of Division Headquarters was Charge of Quarters. Headquarters had to be staffed around the clock and, in the off hours, an Officer of the Day and a Charge of Quarters were on duty. That meant sleeping on a cot, etc., and also getting the next day off to "recuperate." We took turns at this duty. Our skills for performing our functions were slowly being honed and we became adept at our routines. We came out of our training ready for overseas duty (we were mentally "up" for that) and, in a sense, raring to go. We knew that the infantry regiments were well trained; we had confidence in our leaders. As glider troopers, we were in a sense second-class citizens in a division which by April '43 had become two-thirds parachutist. However, our morale was high—all systems "go."

Unfortunately, our bend-the-rules attitude jumped up and bit us when the G-3 section was hit by scandal, which I'll get to shortly, and M/Sgt. Dorant, Staff Sgt. Wilhelm and Sgt. Witty were summarily busted from their rank and transferred to the 325th Glider Infantry. As time wore on with its ramifications, Dorant rejoined us in Italy, and Wilhelm just before Normandy. Witty was never heard from again.

And so ends our training and preparation for war. Our leisure time on base centered around a cluster of frame buildings near the parade grounds and the Headquarters buildings. There was the PX where you could buy gifts, insignia, cigarettes (at ridiculously low prices), needles and thread and other odds and ends. It was also the place where beer with limited alcoholic content was sold in the evening hours. Even with the 3.2 content, the beer was intoxicating enough and every night there were scores of soldiers there drinking as fast as they could, the trick being to pile the empty cans in pyramid fashion to see which table could erect the highest structure. It was also a place where tempers inevitably got the upper hand and the MP's were frequently called in to quiet the incipient riots.

There was a theater which could seat about a thousand and was used during the days (particularly when it rained) for lectures and training films. There was the occasional touring USO troupe, but most of the time it was used for evening movies. When the theater was dark, during the changing of films, etc., the men used to play ack-ack. Guys would blow up condoms, tie the end and launch them in the air to cries of "Air raid!" Immediately, dozens of flashlights would materialize in the darkness, their projected beams seeking the floating items. When a flashlight would fix onto one of the "aircraft," there would be loud shouts of "Ack-Ack, Ack-ack!" and literally dozens of lit cigarettes thrown at it. Oddly enough, every now and then a cigarette would down the condom amidst thunderous cheering. Many times, this part of the show was better than the movie.

While on the subject of cigarettes, almost everybody smoked. On breaks, during training or a march or whatever, the standard command was, "Take a break, you can smoke." Later, when in combat and living on packaged and/or canned rations, each packaged meal, when broken open, contained a small pack of smokes. Chewing tobacco and cigars were also available from time to time for those who sought those pleasures, but not as readily as cigarettes. While in training at Bragg, they were very cheap. Later, when overseas, the amount I got through the army was augmented by those I received in packages from Alice. I was never without.

A lot of drinking was also done in town by many of the men in notorious spots like the Town Pump, where nightly brawls were expected. The men from particular outfits would choose their own bar and congregate there; the brawls would break out when there was more than one outfit "claiming" the bar. This violence seemed to be tacitly condoned by the powers that be as necessary letting off steam by men being trained to be (let's face it) killers.

Next to the theater on the post was an indoor area I refer to as the lounge—an area where there were sofas, etc., a place to congregate. There was a small restaurant where hamburgers and hot dogs were available. Also, a library and several juke boxes. In the evening hours, one had to be in Class A uniform to use this area; in other words, dressed up. Songs like "White Christmas" got a heavy play on the jukebox. What I remember most about the scene was how good everybody looked, lean and fit. One thing about the airborne, they looked like they belonged in the uniforms they wore. In this atmosphere, men from the 82d and 101st co-existed comfortably, something that never happened off the base.

A word about the barracks. They were uniform two story buildings, arranged in rows with the company street in between the rows. As I recall, there was room for about 20–24 cots on each floor. There was a large open latrine area in which there were no enclosures around the toilets, a number of sinks and a shower room. It took some getting used to, but eventually everyone did. There was a furnace room, reachable from the outside and I think the heat system was forced air. There was, of course, no air conditioning. Everything was utilitarian and sufficient to the purpose.

There was a great distinction in the early days of the Division between the parachute element and the glider. The parachutists were volunteers and went through a very vigorous procedure to get their wings, including intensive physical conditioning. They also were paid an additional $50 a month, which doubled the pay of a private. The glidermen, in contrast, were newer in the army, not as well conditioned physically and had normal pay. At first, the parachute components were only a third of the Division but in January of 1943 that changed to two thirds, thereby making the glider troops a minority in more ways than one. This problem of supposed second-class citizenship caused by the elite nature of the jumpers vs. the glidermen existed for almost two years, until the 325th Glider Infantry showed its mettle in Normandy.

Ridgway tried to combat this by authorizing the design of the cap patch to include a glider and parachute to be worn by all, replacing the parachute patch, which had been worn only by the parachutists. There was much complaint about this from the parachutists. The final leveling action was to equip all the men with the distinctive jump boots which, along with jump suits, were the pride of the parachutists. The jump suits were discarded as they wore out. Everybody was equipped with jump boots after the Normandy campaign.

But before wrapping up our days at Fort Bragg and departure for overseas, a scandal struck G-3. In April of '43, we knew we were headed overseas. We, at one point, were sealed in, meaning no one could enter or leave our area without special permission. It became known to us in G-3 that we were going to be staged for overseas duty out of Camp Edwards on Cape Cod in Massachusetts. Not known was that surveillance was put on the comings and goings of key personnel, including us at G-3. It developed that Witty had notified his family by mail and Wilhelm his wife by telephone of the impending move. At the same time Dorant defied the physical seal on the camp and had gone off on one of his amorous adventures.

All three were summarily busted to Private and transferred from Headquarters to the 325th Glider Infantry. So we were heading for overseas minus our three most senior NCO's. No longer was the G-3 section the star of Headquarters!

5

SHIPPING OUT

Training was over and we were on our way overseas. Everybody pared down their amount of accumulated stuff and was supposed to take along only what was prescribed in a list and which was to be fitted into two barracks bags, labeled "A" and "B." Most men stretched the list somewhat; for example, I brought along my Brownie camera with which I took some pictures in Africa and Normandy. (Later, in Germany, I traded a liberated pistol for a better camera.)

We also had the opportunity to have some crates built to our specifications which would be used in the campaigns to come to carry our working equipment. After some discussion we settled on a number of crates sized about 2-1/2 by 2-1/2 by 6 feet, equipped with hasps and locks and heavy duty handles. Little did we know how useless these would prove to be. When full they weighed a couple of hundred pounds, had to be handled by two to three men, and did not lend themselves to be dumped into a jeep trailer. In the event, they stayed with our rear echelon throughout the war and we carried our working supplies in ammunition boxes which were of a size that could be handled quickly by one man and loaded and unloaded easily from our vehicles—either jeep, jeep trailer or truck.

For some reason, in one of those many incidents labeled SNAFU, we went from Ft. Bragg to Camp Edwards on Cape Cod in Massachusetts, stayed there about two weeks and then came back to New York from where we embarked for North Africa. The only explanation I can come up with is that perhaps we were slated to leave from Boston but orders were changed to New York after we'd already gone to Massachusetts. Anyway, after about two weeks on Cape Cod, we left for our embarkation point—Staten Island in New York Harbor.

The train taking us to Camp Edwards passed through Penn Station and took the Long Island Railroad tunnels to Sunnyside, Queens, on its way to the Hellgate Bridge and the New Haven tracks to New England. In the Sunnyside yards, it was night and we were standing there for about an hour before moving on, producing a melodramatic moment because, only a few blocks away, behind one of those twinkling lights that shown from apartment windows, was Alice spending an evening wondering, no doubt, where I was, and probably writing one of her daily letters which were to be an anchor for me during the ensuing years.

The weeks at Camp Edwards were uneventful but full of rumors and speculation. For once, we at HQ did not know when and where we were going. The G-3 section was also under a cloud because of the three non-coms who'd been busted and transferred due to the various breaches of security. Those of us who remained were walking around with a little less than our usual confidence. Colonel Boyd must also have taken some heat because of the actions of his men and was uncharacteristically glum.

Just before the final preparations for leaving Ft. Bragg, the Division had received an infusion of about the same size as the one I came with from Camp Upton. This time it was from the Chicago area. G-3 had received three men from this group, Lange, Pritikin and Rohr. It was a good thing, too, otherwise we would have been seriously shorthanded.

Bill Mehrholz was chosen to take over Dorant's spot and Graddy Richard was promoted to Wilhelm's. Mehrholz was a little older than the rest of the other guys, came from Chicago and had worked for the Columbia Banknote Company. He was a good typist and at home in routine office functions. He was deliberate in manner, quite serious, balding, and very easy to get along with. He and I put our pup tent halves together in Africa and shared this arrangement for the period between arriving in Oujda and the invasion of Sicily.

Graddy Richard was a very elegant guy, a lawyer from Louisville, and a member of a family that was high in the management of the Brown-Forman whiskey manufacturers. He had a strong and pleasant personality and was truly liked and respected by all. His expertise was as a draftsman and he and I shared those duties. He, like me, wanted to apply to Officers Candidate School, but as it turned out, all such applications were on hold from the beginning of 1943 when we were slated for overseas shipment. The applications opened up anew when we got to Ireland and we both put in ours. Again, fate was against us because the officer in charge of interviewing the applicants, Colonel Barrett, the Division Inspector General, was ill for months and didn't conduct his interviews until the Spring of 1944 and we were in England. Too late—we were preparing for Normandy and, once again, all OCS activity was on hold.

Just before the end of May 1944, only a few weeks before the invasion, Graddy was specially requested, through the War Department, as a result of pressure put on by influential members of his family, to go back to the States for enrollment in the Judge Advocate General School. We all missed him. As mentioned, he was very elegant and also meticulous in his work and conduct. His personal grooming was legendary. When we filled out our OCS applications in Ireland, we both approached Captain Gerard for individual letters of recommendation, which he gave us. On Richard's he noted the deep impression the aforementioned personal grooming had on him. "In the dusty conditions of Africa, Sgt. Richard's clothes were always neat and his shoes polished," he wrote, meaning it as a compliment, I assume. But Graddy considered it as damning with faint praise, indeed, and was quite angry and upset. I agreed with him.

At Camp Edwards I was selected to be on the advance party to the embarkation point at Staten Island representing Division HQ and also HQ Co. Each battalion, or possibly company, was represented by a man whose function was to familiarize himself with the area on the ship where his unit would be billeted and to meet his unit on their arrival at the Port of Embarkation and lead the men to their quarters. Why I was chosen I have no idea, but it turned out to be fortunate for me because that led to my being co-opted by the small army group "running" the transport. I ate well, had the freedom of the ship, and did not have to sleep down in the bowels of the vessel as did the rest of Division HQ.

So then came the excitement and realization of actually being on a dock in a harbor about to board a ship to lead us (finally) to a war zone. Which one we did not know, but since we were on the East Coast the odds were Europe. Although there was still some fighting going on in Africa, somehow we didn't feel we were headed in that direction. It is difficult to explain, after so many years, the excitement, nervousness and thrill (also fear) that took hold. Also a certain elation and self-consciousness in step. It was kind of like a two-phased scene, one in which I was taking part and the other looking at myself on stage in the role of my life.

I had started to develop at that time a way of evaluating whatever situation I was in so as to minimize the immediate dangers. For instance, when I joined the Army in 1942, it was not known that the big invasion of Europe would not take place for almost two years. I was going through training fully expecting that by the time we were ready, that large step would be taken by others. If we had known that we would be in every major engagement in Europe (with the exception of the break-out from Normandy and subsequent over-running of France) we would have been a glum and disbelieving group indeed.

The ship we crammed onto was named the *Washington* and was a commandeered German merchant ship that had been seized by the U.S. and prepared for transporting troops. This was to be the ship's first use as such and it had been designed to accommodate as many men as could possibly be squeezed into it. Down to the lowest level of the ship, and there were probably eight levels as I recall, all the compartments were rigged out with three-level cots—very claustrophobic, particularly for those assigned to one of the lower levels as I soon found out we were.

The ship was designated as an Army (as distinguished from Navy) transport and was manned by a merchant marine crew. The Army Transportation Command placed a crew of one officer and six enlisted men on board to serve as liaison between the merchant crew and the Army passengers. There was also a small U.S. Navy detachment who manned the complement of guns mounted on deck. When I arrived on the *Washington* and received the data about where my unit was to be located, I got to talking with the Staff Sergeant who was giving out the billeting assignments and was the ranking NCO of the Army detachment. When he learned I could type, he told me he could use some help and, if I wanted to, I could be relieved of the boredom of the trip, eat good meals (served by waiters) and sleep top-side. Needless to say, I jumped at the offer and was given a green armband which gave me the run of the ship. (Military Police were stationed at key hatches and bulkheads so as to confine the men to their prescribed areas). So as a result of my agreeing to help out, the only time I stayed on F-Deck was to stow my barracks bags on a cot and come back to retrieve them when we arrived at Casablanca.

The ship was so crowded that only half the men could be above decks at any given time, so a schedule was established sharing time between above and below decks. Good water was at a premium—salt water flowed in the wash-up areas. Meals were served in a large hall with waist high benches (or tables) and were eaten while standing. I only had one such meal and that was enough—OK, if one liked hard boiled eggs, which I didn't. From time to time, from my exalted perch, I would visit with the guys when they were sprawled out on the deck to shoot the breeze. Needless to say, I sensed considerable resentment over the cushy job I had latched onto.

When we were loaded on the ship, I thought that being in the harbor no enemy could reach us there. When we sailed—well, we were still within spitting distance of land, and when we were at sea we were in the middle of a comforting convoy, and surely nothing could touch us there either. Actually, I discovered through reading in later years that April 1943 was the height of the U-boat menace and that they had lurked and done damage within sight of the U.S.

There was a small office aboard ship assigned to the detachment I was now working with and I reported there each day. We had the 504th on board with us as well as special troops and some artillery. The Division was transported, as I recall, on three ships, one of which was the *Monterey*, which in peacetime was an elegant cruise ship. General Ridgway was on board with us.

Also on board was a large group of replacements—almost of regimental strength—who came along in anticipation of the casualties we would take. Because of the special nature of our division—airborne— we would not get replacements from the same channels as did the regular infantry divisions. For some reason, this group was given the name EGB and had been billeted in Camp Shanks in New York prior to joining us in New York Harbor. For many unknown reasons, the complete complement did not show up, either being AWOL or in hiding or whatever—rumors abounded and part of the job we had in our small group was to verify who on the list we were provided actually were on board. It took days before we had an accurate list. And the label stuck—anybody who was part of that group was always referred to as, "Oh, yeah, he was an EGB."

Shortly after leaving port we were told we were headed for Africa, which was kind of a letdown because we had thought, or perhaps hoped, we were headed for England. The strategists among us couldn't figure it out, little as we knew of the grand strategy that was developing to strike Europe through Italy (called the "soft underbelly" of Europe by a persuasive Churchill). The cross-Channel strike at France would be held off for more than another year.

Outside of all the rumors, the voyage settled down to a boring routine for most of the men, the most important events being the twice a day meals and alternating being on the deck and below. We were told when we could smoke or not when on deck, and particular care was enforced against showing any light on deck during hours of darkness. Dumping anything overboard was absolutely forbidden. Card games were all over the place and there was talk of one very big crap game somewhere in the bowels of the ship but, since traveling around the vessel was prohibited, that was probably only rumor.

Besides working in the small office, I occupied my time writing a long letter detailing all the features of the ship and the convoy, and to my dismay, saw that almost all of it was excised by an over-zealous censor. It was something we now had to get used to—someone reading our personal mail. Later in the war, we would write, address and seal the letters and hand it to one of our officers to "censor" which he would do by signing on the envelope without reading the contents.

The first day out of New York there was an "incident." We were in a large convoy with a corresponding-sized group of Navy ships bristling with anti-submarine devices. There was an old World War I battleship and a full complement of destroyers. There were probably thirty ships in all in the convoy. In broad daylight our ship suddenly lost power and stopped. We were riding the swells helplessly and noiselessly in the Atlantic, not far out of New York, while the German

U-Boat campaign was in full bore. The rest of the convoy steamed on and we were left wallowing in the water being circled by a single destroyer. Fortunately, the problem was fixed; we steamed on and eventually found our way back into the convoy. The fact that the convoy was ready to leave us was evidence of the grim realities—laggards would not be permitted to bring down the whole group.

The battleship in the convoy had a bi-plane sort of dangling on a platform off to the side of the main deck, and from tine to time it would be catapulted into flight and the pilot would circle the convoy looking for traces of enemy submarines. On finishing the overflight the pilot would land on its floats (it was a sea plane), taxi over to the side of the battleship and be picked up by sort of a hook arrangement. It looked kind of dangerous, particularly in rough seas. Sure enough, one day when we were watching it, the plane touched down onto the sea, taxied over to the side of the battlewagon, and suddenly disappeared! As with us, when we were disabled, no visible effort was made to locate the plane or rescue its crew—the convoy just sailed on.

Now, since this was happening probably five to six hundred yards from where we were looking (and we were only idly observing the scene), the sea being rough and the swells high, it wasn't universally agreed among us that the plane had sunk. I was able to confirm that it had indeed been lost when I had dinner later with my benefactors. But as may be guessed, when I was with my men the next time and related this information, it was greeted with the skepticism that was born of resentment and other emotions because of the job I had fortuitously attained on the ship.

On another occasion, while having supper on the upper deck, a bell similar to a doorbell rang and everybody, except me, dropped their forks, grabbed their life jackets and scurried out of the compact dining room. I was left there, slightly perplexed, and finished my meal. Sometime later the others returned and I found out there had been a submarine sighting, that the destroyer escorts had dropped depth charges and now everything seemed to be "as you were." The next day I once again made my way to the guys on the deck and related the story of the night before and, to a man, no one bought it. My words were greeted with eye-rolling and mutterings about what I was "full of." Another example of the complex system of rumors, "shoot the messenger" and the relative positions of those in and out of the know.

The weather on the crossing had been fine and excitement grew as we neared the end of the journey. At last we sighted land and it was Casablanca on the Atlantic coast of French Morocco. We did not have to pass through the Straits of Gibraltar, which was a relief. We disembarked and marched to a nearby open area where we set up our pup tents for a stay of short duration while arrangements were concluded for our departure along the route of the Atlas Mountains to Oujda, also in Morocco. We were able to get a few hours to visit the city of Casablanca. The strongest memory I have is of white buildings, men clothed in robes rather than pants and shirts, the absence of women on the streets, and the burro, or jackass, which was the seeming universal method of transportation.

The trip across North Africa was via train and we were loaded onto ancient cars, some with hard benches and some labeled "40 hommes/8 cheveux," which were tiny freight cars. Actually they were more comfortable than the cars with seats, because there were some bales of hay which could be strewn about and the trip could be taken in a reclining position. The cars moved so slowly that it seemed possible to get out of the train and walk alongside without losing any ground. It was a hot, boring, uncomfortable couple of days until finally we got to our area in Oujda and our first introduction to what the word "desert" means.

6

NORTH AFRICA

Africa was hot and dusty, full of tiny scorpions that stung, persistent flies that appeared in clouds whenever food was exposed, and generally miserable conditions. We pitched our camp in an area that was north of the Sahara but nonetheless a desert, with the principal foliage being scraggly cactus. The ground was hard, whitish and grainy, almost impossible to dig into. Latrines for the men had to be blasted out of the earth with dynamite, and the warning shout "Fire in the hole!" signifying an ensuing blast was common and became kind of a mantra.

We set up rows of pup tents, each joining with another man and his shelter half to make a tent which became home for a couple of months. Of course, we learned some ways to mitigate the conditions. We secured thin-necked clay jugs from the Arabs for our water. Outside the pup tent we (Bill Mehrholz and I) laboriously dug a hole about two feet deep. The bottom of it we lined with straw. The drinking water supply was treated against the many rampant diseases and hung in large bags called Lister Bags in strategic locations.

As hot as it became in the day, so it was cool at night, requiring the use of blankets. And the water in the Lister Bags cooled off as well. So we learned to fill our water jug (about two-quart capacity) early in the morning when it was cold, wet the outside of the jug, wrap the jug in a couple of towels, place it in the straw-lined hole and cover it with more straw. This provided a cool supply of water during the day, when we were near the tent—which was only some of the time. Once in a while we were able to latch onto a couple of oranges which we also stashed in the hole for a real treat.

We heard about the Sirocco, then found out what it was. The days would start off cool, then relentlessly begin to heat up about 9 AM. By noon, the heat and sun were brutal and by two in the afternoon the temperature would be hovering about 110 degrees. At 3 PM, almost without fail, came the Sirocco, a fierce wind blowing clouds of blinding sand from the desert toward the Mediterranean in the north. The sand got into everything, including one's mouth, nose, eyes and ears. It was impossible to do anything except go for cover when the wind was blowing. After about an hour it would die down and taper off until dusk when the chill of the evening started.

We had arrived in North Africa while there was still some mopping up activity going on to complete the surrender of the remains of Rommel's Africa Corps. We waved to the occasional convoy of sunburned and lean British 7th Armoured troops (the famous Desert Rats) that passed by, noting their weathered look and scruffy uniforms, which included shorts rather than trousers. We could tell they had been through the hard times that we were just embarking on. We were duly impressed by their appearance.

But we were there for training and, as we soon found out, our objective was the island of Sicily, sitting as it does below the toe of the Italian boot, and only a short hop by plane from the northern coast of Africa. Because of the brutal climate conditions, the Division was forced to institute a training schedule where the main field work was done at night rather than in the impossible heat of the day. Airborne training was sharply curtailed because of the wind and the rock-strewn terrain—too many injuries were sustained.

We had a lot of re-organizing to do within G-3. Mehrholz, Richard and I, the oldest in service, were augmented by Pritikin, Lange and Rohr, who had joined us in the early part of 1943. All of them were promoted to T/5 (equivalent to Corporal) and then, in Africa, we received two new men. Both Privates, they were Linden Morse from upstate New York and Ray Jungclas from Cincinnati, thus bulking up the enlisted group to eight men. During the training phase in the North African desert, our group had adequate size. Mehrholz had taken over quite well and, gradually, the problems associated with the busting of Dorant and the others receded.

Marv Pritikin, of the group who joined us at the turn of the year, hailed from Chicago and was some years younger than the rest of us. Like me, Marv was Jewish and, fortunately for all of us, his family had a grocery store somewhere back in the States and Marv's packages from home were legendary—like manna from heaven, and he generously shared everything. He became very friendly with Richard and helped give our group a pleasant, good-humored tone. Marv got quite sick with some kind of a gland problem before Normandy so did not take part in that campaign, but served with us in Sicily and Italy and after Normandy to the end of the war. All that good food made him sloppily overweight and not in great shape—his appearance not helped by his premature baldness. But we loved those packages! Marv could be relied on to do a creditable job keeping the G-3 Journal which formed the day-by-day record of the Division's activities and became the basis for all the After Action Reports. He also gave a hand with the midnight Situation Reports (while we were in action) and accompanying overlays, which were run off on the hectograph jelly pads. His rank for most of the war was buck Sergeant (3 stripes).

Another man who had joined us in early 1943 was Jack Rohr, from Freeport, Illinois. I guess every group has a Rohr, the malcontent and complainer, and truculent to boot. Jack was never happy, hardly ever joined in whatever merriment there might be, and was really a difficult guy to have along. His only joy seemed to come from his reminiscing about the girl he left behind in Illinois, whose name was Nellie and who was training to be a nurse. Jack really resented the Army and was not made for it. His skill was as a draftsman and he was used mainly to compose and produce the evening Situation Report. In the Spring of 1945, when a new Table of Organization was developed and our size expanded, Jack was promoted to Sergeant.

G-3 had a large pyramidal tent for our working area. We rolled up the sides early in the day until the coming of the inevitable wind, then we dropped them. We had never been in the field before, so we had to start getting used to not operating out of a building, acclimating to poor light at night and little or no furniture to work on. We had a couple of plain folding tables, some folding chairs, and the rest we improvised, using the crates we had brought along to stow our things in as seats, desks, dining tables, etc. We had a gasoline fueled Coleman lantern for use at night, which we supplemented by flashlights. As the troops trained in the desert, so we were learning as well.

Strategically, most of us were of the opinion that at the same time we would invade Sicily there would be a simultaneous landing in France. None of us believed the Allied effort would be confined to the Mediterranean. However, we became engrossed in our planning and only did not know the exact date of the action.

During this period we entertained some of the heavy brass. There was a full division review for the corps commander, General George Patton, who appeared together with the DeGaullist general of whatever French forces there were (not many). It was in the usual heat, and Patton favored us with one of his "kick 'em in the balls" speeches addressed to the vast ocean of men drawn up in the desert sun. He hadn't achieved the celebrity which later came to him. We knew he was an armored general, a tanker through and through. His inspirational speech was met mainly with shrugged shoulders and eyerolling on the part of the men.

We also had a visit from Eisenhower, who was the theater commander and for whom we did not put on a division review—one had been enough. For Ike, all the Division's field grade officers (major and up) were assembled, along with one honor guard infantry company from the 504th. Looking at Eisenhower, as I did from the sidelines, he gave a different impression from the photos one saw, which were usually head shots featuring the famous grin. When seen full length one saw a well put together, almost aggressive figure. He made no friends when he confined his remarks to the observation that when he drove into the Division area with his four-star shield on his car, he passed men who did not salute. I'm sure Ridgway was delighted.

So much for the visits. Life was going on and we were getting toughened, so maybe the rigors of the terrain and weather were serving a purpose. The men were getting meaner, with fights breaking out all over the place. One enterprising battalion commander came up with the idea of bayonet practice on live animals with confiscated goats being used as the "enemy."

In addition to the weather conditions, there were medical problems. Jaundice, malaria and dysentery abounded and we were cautioned to drink only the water supplied in the Lister Bags. We also took Atabrine pills each day, which slowly turned us all a sickly shade of yellow. Everyone had dysentery, which was spread by the flies that hovered between the latrines and the eating areas. It was impossible to find a place not infested with flies while eating, and the usual system was to fan the flies away with one hand while eating with the other.

Mail was our tether to home. I tried to write every day but it was difficult not to be repetitive because that's the way our life was. On the other hand, I was fortunate in receiving mail constantly because Alice also wrote once a day and her letters were long and newsy. It was during this time that I found out we were to become parents, a miracle to happen sometime toward the end of 1943. Of course, all of that burden was going to fall on Alice, who was determined to work as long as she could before giving birth. Much of our correspondence from then on was about the impending child.

The day of the Sicilian invasion was drawing inevitably closer. We had one delightful break from the deadening routine. Trips were made with about 25 men at a time out of the desert, over the hills that ringed the coast some few miles inland from the sea, to the sea itself where we had the opportunity for a day of swimming in the Mediterranean. The slopes of the hills toward the sea were in full bloom with orchards and fields of grain, quite a contrast to the desert on the other side. We heard that all of North Africa had once been verdant but had lapsed into infertility because of denuding the area of trees.

And then I was called in and told that I was going to be included on the advance group (again) to Sicily. General Ridgway was going to be on the same ship as the Army commander (Patton would be so designated on the day of the invasion) and he was taking a small group with him, including his aide, Captain Faith; his driver, Sgt. Farmer; the Chief of Staff, Colonel Eaton; the G-2, Colonel Lynch; the Intelligence Sgt. Spotswood; the G-3, Colonel Boyd; and me, as the Operations Sergeant. Spotswood was a Master Sgt. and I was a T/4, equivalent to a three-striper. Bill Mehrholz did not have the skills to work on maps and I have no idea why I was chosen before Richard, who out-ranked me and was also nominally a draftsman. Not that I minded. I was elated at the opportunity. The rest of the section, officers and men, would follow up some days after the invasion and, in the event, would come about 4 or 5 days after D-Day, landing, to my best recollection, on a

Sicilian airfield. In this invasion, gliders were used by the British on their end of the front; because of shortages of gliders and tow planes, we did not use any.

And so, in early July we were driven to Algiers, the embarkation port. We found it to be exciting and bustling with troops and activity, and we loaded onto the USS *Monrovia*, which was fitted with all kinds of communication gear as the command ship of the Seventh Army and also of the fleet carrying us to battle. Admiral Hewitt, in charge of the fleet, was on board.

It was the 3rd of July, 1943.

7

ON THE MEDITERRANEAN

It was exhilarating. The piers and the roads leading to them were bustling with activity as, over the next few days, truck convoy after convoy came down the dusty streets to the docks, unloaded their cargo of troops, who reassembled and struggled, loaded down with battle gear, up the gangplanks to their respective ships. Some were taken out to the anchored ships in small bobbing and pitching landing craft. Our little group had loaded relatively early so we had ringside seats to observe the bustling scene as it developed.

We also had hoped to get to visit Algiers, but once on the ship we were sealed aboard and all we could do was look and speculate on what the city would be like. The city was the principal one in North Africa and the headquarters of the Allied Command under Eisenhower. It was also the scene of an immensely popular film of a few years prior starring Hedy Lamarr and Charles Boyer, at which time the Western world became acquainted with the concept of the romanticized Casbah, the "native" quarter, supposedly inaccessible and highly dangerous to outsiders. The city fanned out from the harbor in semi-circular fashion with a continuous rise to the outward hills. From the water, it looked shining white and welcoming in the sun. But for us it was, if ever, to be visited another day.

The *Monrovia*, our ship, was a Navy troop carrier, outfitted as a command ship, but operated with a full Navy crew as compared with the *Washington*, which took us overseas from New York crewed by the merchant marine. The ship had only limited armament, some 5" cannon and a number of 40mm and 20mm antiaircraft guns.

This was our first close exposure to the Navy and the first thing that struck us Army guys was how young the sailors looked. And clean. And we also noted their superior food, which was served cafeteria style and eaten at tables (!) sitting down. While aboard, we of course had the same routine. And we noted that, among other things, beans were always served at breakfast.

I was assigned a bunk somewhere below decks. Before leaving Oujda I was informed that I was to drive a command car across the beach. I had never driven the vehicle before and sought it out below decks and stowed some of my stuff in it. A command car can be described as an over-sized jeep which rode quite high off the ground. It was used extensively in the States throughout the Army in the early days but never took hold overseas (it was relatively useless compared to a jeep) and was gradually withdrawn from service.

Among our individual possessions were supplies of Atabrine tablets for purifying water, sulfa powder as a general disinfectant, a parachute first aid kit which included morphine and bandages, and a supply of ammunition and hand grenades. We each had a shelter half which could be laid out on the ground for sleeping, for use as half a tent or as a simple shelter against rain. I kind of figured that toilet paper might be a problem so I relieved the Navy of two rolls, which I stuffed in my baggage within the command car. I also cut off a length of about 3/16ths diameter smooth rope from a large roll, instinctively feeling I might have use for it. The toilet paper stayed with me, in diminishing quantity, through the various campaigns to come and the rope was absolutely indispensable from time to time as well.

I sat in the car to get a feel for its dimensions and gear shift, etc. I knew the car would have protective grease applied to it because it was to be driven through salt water and also that one of the first things that would happen on landing would be the removal of this special protective coating.

In retrospect, it is amazing how much of what I was to do was done without any rehearsal at all. We would leave the ship by climbing down one of those scary looking rope nets into a moving landing craft; I would be mated with this car and then drive it off the landing craft through whatever surf there was to the de-greasing station. None of this was rehearsed. The command car and I were given a load number (I don't remember exactly—something like 47) and when that number was called I was to report to a designated debarkation spot on the deck with full equipment, ready to climb down the ladder. I was able to stow most of my gear into the command car but still would have a light field pack on my back, a carbine over my shoulder and an uncomfortable helmet on when my time came to leave the *Monrovia*. But I am a little ahead of the story.

The atmosphere was almost like the start of a vacation, full of anticipation. The sight of the tremendous build-up of men, vehicles and ships was heartening and also fed a certain sense of pride and mission. The fleet spread out across the harbor, large ships and small, with the gray, sleek fighting ships off in the distance as our guardians. Most of the ships flew small barrage balloons which were airship shaped, tethered to the sterns of ships by a wire and flown some 100 feet or so above the fleet. The purpose, as I learned, was to prevent enemy aircraft from making low level attacks against the fleet because the random pattern of tether wires would snag any intruding plane.

Although we were in the harbor for days, boredom did not set in because of the magnitude of the gathering fleet. We spent time observing, speculating, eating and enjoying the "time off" and good food and the nightly movies. Most of the men I talked with were "up" for the event and morale was very high. There was a thrill in being part of this enormous effort.

From this distance in time, I can no longer remember whether we were at sea for two or three nights. I believe it was three, which would mean we left Algiers on the 7th of July. The huge convoy took hours to assemble in sections and we headed out to sea in the afternoon.

To give us, the Army personnel, something to do, the Navy found assignments for us as back-ups to the Navy crew. Spotswood and I were assigned to the 40mm guns which were located on the hurricane deck, an area about 25 feet square just below the bridge of the *Monrovia*. There were four guns, one at each corner of the deck, and a three-man crew operated each gun. We were given a brief primer in the operation of the equipment but knew in our hearts that, in an emergency, these guns would be operated by sailors, not us. Anyway we accepted the assignment happily and reported to the deck when our watch was called.

Little did we know when given the duty that we would be in the company of the big brass, because the hurricane deck was the traditional area where the ship's captain and officers would catch a breath of air and a smoke when on a break from their duties. And so it was that General Patton and his staff, Admiral Hewitt, a handful of reporters who were on the ship, and others, including our General Ridgway, materialized on the deck while we were standing our watch.

Patton was resplendent in his cavalry breeches, boots and silver buckled belt, from which dangled his signature brace of ivory handled revolvers. Up close he had an appearance which belied his fearsome reputation. He was blessed with a pink-to-florid complexion, a high-pitched voice and was a little corpulent. He walked (or strutted?) about this little area, rocking on the balls of his feet, followed by his coterie, while he carried on a running commentary. Obviously he was in a light-hearted mood, because his remarks were greeted by bursts of laughter from the assembled officers and others. Except for Ridgway, that is. I noticed, and confirmed with Spotswood later, that Ridgway distanced himself from the group, did not take part in the sycophantic laughter, and generally managed to position himself on the opposite side of the deck from where Patton was. And then Patton made a point to speak to each of us manning the guns. "Where are you from, soldier?" he asked, with a smile. "New York City, sir," said I. "Good," he said, and passed on to the next man.

So much for my exposure to greatness. Over the years, I have become an amateur student of WWII and one cannot do that without pondering George S. Patton. He most certainly was the most successful offensive-minded army commander we had and showed his mettle during the breakout from Normandy the following year. That was his plus. He was aware of the power of good public relations and was always receptive to the press, garnering a much better reputation than the other ETO commanders, including his superior, General Bradley. How he would have done if faced with a situation having elements of stalemate or of having to deal face to face with our Allies, the British, is not known. He also committed the unthinkable by actually striking soldiers on two different occasions in Sicily—men who were possibly suffering from battle fatigue and were in Aid Stations along with wounded soldiers. When this news broke, it caused Patton to be relieved of command and "put on ice" until August 1944 when the Third Army became operational in France. Speculating on what might have happened without these incidents is intriguing.

The first day at sea was consciously the beginning of a great adventure, full of heightened anticipation for all. When I found the opportunity, I located Colonel Boyd and asked whether this was the only operation going on or if it was happening at the same time as a cross-Channel invasion of France from Britain. I was disappointed when told that this was "it" for the time being. In my ignorance of matters of scale and possibility, I had hoped there would be that strike as well as ours in the Mediterranean. So much for amateur planning.

Later that same day, Boyd had me paged and when I reported he advised me that there was a Brigadier General Al Weydemeyer on board "from Washington," and instructed me to go to his stateroom and mark up his map case with the projected drop zones of the various elements of our division. As I found out later, Weydemeyer was specifically sent from the War Department to observe the operation and file his report in which the planning and execution would be evaluated. He later became very prominent when he was sent to replace General Stillwell in the Pacific Theater at the end of the war.

I knocked on his door and was greeted by a tall, handsome man and told him what I had been sent to do. A word about the standard Army map case: It was book-like, opening up to two letter-sized halves, each in the form of a stiff envelope with the opposing inside surfaces covered with thick transparent sheets. Maps could be slipped under these sheets, or one map could bridge underneath the two, and then the transparent sheets could be written on with grease pencils, which normally were supplied in red, black and blue. I centered the maps, which he had, and drew in the drop zone areas as circles and, using the Army symbols, noted which units were scheduled for each zone.

He thanked me profusely and, as I started to leave, he hesitated, stopped me and then pointed to his footlocker. "Open it up," he said, which I did and noted that the entire top tray was filled with Clark candy bars! "Take one," and when I did, he said "take another." This I did and then thanked him and left the room, thinking all the while of the various orderlies and privates who had been lugging this foot locker loaded with the general's supply of candy bars all over the place. (I didn't return the candy, however—it was a real treat.)

Also aboard the *Monrovia* was Douglas Fairbanks, Jr., the son of the cinematic hero of my youth, and also a Hollywood star. He was in the Navy, wore the two bars of a Lieutenant (equivalent to an Army captain) and was rumored to be involved in some kind of hush-hush operation. I ran into him while passing through a bulkhead aboard ship and he gave a kind of self-conscious smile. Ships passing in the night.

The second day the weather took a turn for the worse and by nightfall we were in a full force gale. As the day progressed, the barrage balloons started taking alarming dips and swoops, actually becoming somewhat of a menace as sometimes they came close to striking the ships' superstructures and decks. They were then hauled in and secured to the decks. Someone had told me that the way to beat seasickness was to stand on deck and look at the horizon and, conversely, not to look at the rail or any other feature of the boat which, viewed against the sea, would accentuate the rolling and pitching of the ship. Many on board became sick during the storm but I remembered the advice and stood on deck, holding on while looking out to the horizon. Whether or not that was the reason, I did not get sick and found it rather exhilarating.

Fortunately the weather moderated the next day and by evening (which would be the eve of D-day in Sicily) it became quite calm. Naturally, sleep was hard to come by, since the big day was coming on the morrow. The Navy had managed to move this huge army-at-sea, in its many elements, successfully, and if there were any hostile actions, we on the *Monrovia* did not witness them. The *Monrovia* anchored a couple of miles offshore at Gela, in Sicily, which was the focal point of the seaborne invasion by the First Infantry Division. Toward dawn, the naval bombardment opened up and the invasion was on! Meanwhile, if all went according to plan, the 505th Parachute Infantry and one battalion of the 504th from the 82d Airborne would be landing in the hours of darkness and would be engaging the enemy.

As it became light, from our vantage point on the deck some distance, maybe a mile, offshore, we could make out the smoke and sounds of battle. Reports were not circulated as to progress, but, in the absence of negative news, everyone had the feeling the landings had been a success. No word at all about the airborne landings except we knew that they had happened. As for our little group, General Ridgway and his aide had managed to get taken ashore by landing craft early on. The rest of us were not scheduled to go ashore until the next day, D plus one.

There was little air activity over the anchored fleet. In the distance we could occasionally make out some fighter aircraft flying above and inland of the beaches. It was a nervous morning of watching and waiting, after a night with little or no sleep. Toward about noon Spotswood and I were summoned over the speaker system to report to the main deck, and there was Colonel Eaton, the Division Chief of Staff. His famous words to me were, "How would you like to go ashore?"

There are many ways of giving an order, including, "Get your ass on deck in 30 minutes, ready to leave the ship." Eaton's words carried the same message and, of course, the answer was affirmative. Anyway, the full story was that Colonels Lynch and Boyd were going ashore to make a reconnaissance of the scene, and Spotswood and I would accompany them. We were to leave in half an hour. I dashed below, gathered a canteen of water, a supply of cigarettes, my carbine, rifle belt with ammunition, helmet—went to the head (bathroom in Navy jargon)—and ran up to the disembarking deck, ready to go, nervous as hell.

Then came the adventure of the rope net. As I remember it, the deck was at least 20 feet above the water and over the rail was slung this apparatus of knotted rope forming squares about one foot on each side which you would use to descend to the waiting landing craft below. The rope apparatus follows the contour of the hull until the ship's design creates a gap between the ladder and hull. Where the ladder meets the sea this gap is a couple of feet. The sailors operating the landing craft grab hold of the dangling net/ladder and secure it as best they can so that the climber can find his way into the craft below. The trick is to avoid being crushed between ship and craft.

Going down the ladder was an adventure. As mentioned earlier, we had no training in how to do this. The first thing one noticed in going over the rail was how small the boat below looked and how it was moving up and down and at the same time close to and then away from the Monrovia. Fortunately the ocean was calm and the swells not threatening. Well, there was no way to chicken out, so over I went and down the ladder. It wasn't easy. First of all, there was the helmet which prevented movement of the head in any way except looking down which, I was told, was the worst thing you could do. So I gamely descended, slowly, holding to the rope rungs for dear life, and eventually got to the level of the gunwale (side) of the landing craft. Receiving encouragement from the crew of the little craft and finally reaching out and grabbing a helping hand, I leaped over and fell in a heap on the unforgiving hard bottom of the LCVP (Landing Craft, Vehicle/Personnel) to the amusement of the kids (sailors) who were manning the craft. No matter, I had done it, as did the rest of our small party, and off we went, waving goodbye to Colonel Eaton who was watching us from the deck of the *Monrovia*.

We swept around and the LCVP opened up its engine and we sped (it seemed) shorewise, breasting the swells and coming ever closer to the bluff that marked the shore and the town of Gela on the bluff. So here we were, a gaggle of airborne troops making our first engagement with the enemy in an unrehearsed seaborne landing. Every now and then the front of the craft would rise slightly above the water and descend with a splash, sending a spray of water over us. Everything combined was scary on the one hand and exciting on the other. I think it is in that mode that most men meet their first such experience.

The flat-bottomed LCVP scraped on the beach, the front panel lowered, and we stepped off into the shallow surf, getting our feet wet in the waters off Sicily. Basically, Spotswood and I were bodyguards on this trip, our job being to go wherever Boyd and Lynch went and to be prepared to confront the enemy (who could be German or Italian) if necessary.

We walked up the bluffs into Gela, the sounds of battle being close at hand, but could gather no reports of our 82d troopers. We moved off to the east, winding up in the CP of the First Division, still with no reports of our men who, in some cases were supposed to have landed relatively close to Gela. We did not find Ridgway. When we got hungry during the afternoon, I scrounged some K-rations from some 1st Division men and we wolfed them down. Most of the time Jimmy (Spotswood) and I did relatively little because Lynch and Boyd were busy chatting up their peers in the 1st Division.

Along about nightfall, with our mission having been relatively unsuccessful, we made our way back to the beach and found an LCVP that took us back to the *Monrovia*, climbed up the confounded rope ladder and wearily fell into our bunks. We had made a seaborne landing, spent the day on soil wrested from the enemy, and were still in one piece!

Tomorrow would be the day for our scheduled landing.

8

FIRST CAMPAIGN—SICILY

After a fitful night of sleep, the day dawned bright and we were ready to go. By now we knew that the airborne landings had been made, but there were no accurate reports on their success or failure. I can recall my feelings as being deadened and anxious at the same time.

My scheduled time for leaving the ship was about 11 A.M. I decided to take advantage of the amenities of the *Monrovia* for one last time and, about 9 A.M., I took a shower which was curtailed in a split second when there was a tremendous explosion which caused the ship to wallow about in the calm sea. The cause of this was a bomb dropped from an aircraft, which flew a pattern parallel to the beach and over the anchored invasion fleet and which narrowly missed us, falling into the sea and detonating close to our hull.

I dressed as rapidly as I could. No one wanted to die with his clothes off or while moving one's bowels—this was universal among all the men, akin to the fear of having to go to a hospital in torn underwear. Not that it would make much difference if, in fact, one was wounded or killed. I then made my way topside and awaited my turn to leave the ship. It was a nervous time because there were bombing runs being made against the fleet, although not on a scale large enough to cause serious alarm.

The ship was unloading its beach-bound segments in numerical order and the count kept marching to my number. This time I was to be on my own, alone in the Landing Craft, with no one waving good-bye and encouragement from the deck. My orders were very vague. No assembly point was arranged and I was to "drive around until

I found someone from our party, preferably Colonel Boyd."

"Forty-seven!" That was me and I stood at the debarking point on the deck as the heavy wire ropes dipped into the open hold and came back up and over the deck and rail with my command car. It was lowered into the LCVP and then it was my turn! Somehow, I climbed over the rail and started hand-over-hand, my feet gingerly finding the next lowest rung, slowly descending. Once again I had the dual sensation of doing something and watching myself do it at the same time.

As the Landing Craft were being loaded one at a time, all eyes were on me as I descended, and I was conscious of not wanting to screw up with so many people looking on. Well, similar to the day before, the tricky last maneuvers were negotiated and I was safely in the bottom of the LCVP, courtesy of a number of helping hands. I must have cut a sorry figure because I noticed the sidelong glances the Navy guys were throwing my way and there was little conversation.

As the LCVP surged its way through the waves, the shore came closer and closer, and then we touched down into the chaotic activity of the beach. It seemed much more busy and cluttered than the day before—possibly because now vehicles and supplies were being unloaded as opposed to mainly men.

I mounted the driver's seat of the command car, started the engine (it responded), the forward ramp of the LCVP was lowered, and off I drove into the surf. (Remember, I had never driven this car before.) There were lanes set up on the beach delineated by small flags, and when I reached dry sand I was directed off to a station where a crew of half a dozen men immediately descended on me and the car and rapidly removed the anti-salt water protective coating.

Then I was ordered to get moving and was rapidly directed off the beach. I wound around the face of the bluff along with all the other traffic going upward to the town of Gela. I could see no one I knew and was frantically looking for the familiar double-A shoulder patch of my Division. Everybody, except me, seemed to know where they were going, and every time I thought I'd pull over to get my bearings I was urged along by the MPs.

While this was happening, it was obvious that the town of Gela was in our hands and that the previous day's landings had been successful. There was the noise of artillery fire off in the distance but I was still too new with those sounds to get a feel for how far away or how intense the fire was. There was air activity, which consisted mainly of our fighter planes, P-38's and P-40's overhead. The ubiquitous Thunderbolts and Mustangs were to come later.

I knew it was projected that we would set up our Command Post somewhere on the bluffs above the sea but not in the town of Gela. So I headed out of town in an eastward direction, cautiously moving into territory that was less and less populated by our troops. Since I had not been directed to go to a particular site, I was about ready to pull over and await developments when I espied on the side of the road waving at me the familiar double A! It was Captain Faith, General Ridgway's aide, who had been separated from him and now joined me as my passenger.

Faith had seen Boyd and Lynch earlier and had an idea of where a projected assembly point was located. We drove around, somehow commandeering a DUKW (amphibious truck), and so became a convoy of two vehicles. When we met Boyd and Lynch, we proceeded to a location above the bluffs and somewhat inland of Gela to set up our Command Post, our first of World War II. It wasn't much. When we all were assembled toward the end of the day, Spotswood and I were the NCO's and the rest were the General and his staff officers. Since this was our first experience where the Division was in contact with the enemy, we were learning by doing. We did not set up a map and would not do so for another couple of days. We did, however, dig ourselves some foxholes and start our journal, keeping records of the various messages and activities.

We knew that the balance of the 504th Regimental Combat Team was coming in on the night of the 11th so messages and warnings about the move were circulated among the troops on the beachhead and in the fleet as well. The flight was planned to come in directly over the fleet and then on a path parallel to the areas just inside the coastline. It was destined to be one of the war's biggest fiascos.

The Luftwaffe had been making occasional runs over the fleet all day, and when night fell the Navy's nerves were on edge. When a tense gunner made out the shape of a lumbering bomber-like aircraft over his ship he opened fire, soon joined by all the other Navy gunners and even anti-aircraft units on shore. They were all firing at a stream of C-

47s carring our 504th Regiment. Dozens of planes went down, and I heard later that some gunners kept shooting at planes that had splashed in the water. The air armada was decimated and some three hundred men lost their lives to the "friendly" fire. It was horrifying to watch and the ramifications of the event affected the use of airborne troops for the rest of the war. It is significant that, outside of the Normandy and Southern France invasions, subsequent airborne tactical forces were used in Europe only in conjunction with British-planned operations.

It was very sobering, but with Ridgway in command the pieces were put together as quickly as possible and we were on our way. The full extent of the tragedy was not circulated or publicized until much later in the war.

In contrast to the disaster that hit the 504th, the activities of the 505th had protected several areas of the beachhead from being over-run in the first two days. The command had been badly scattered in its night drop, but the effect had been to further confuse the enemy with dozens of small actions. At one point Colonel Gavin was able to assemble a group on a height later known as Biazza Ridge and hold off a German armored counterattack on the beaches. It took some doing to retrieve and recontact all our scattered elements, and then the Division was given a new mission—to clear the western and north-western areas of Sicily up to Trapani. This the Division did in a rapid, dusty and victorious series of marches against limited opposition.

We were joined in the early days by the balance of our G-3 group who were flown over and air-landed on captured airfields. Sicily was a breaking-in period for us and we started developing the skills need-ed to operate in battle. We quickly found out the things we needed and those that could be discarded. We put out Situation Reports under time pressure and gradually came to do a passable job. Fortunately for this breaking-in, the battle area assigned to us after the first few days was relatively free from heavy confrontation with the enemy, and what we learned most of all was how to set up our operating location, break it down quickly and move to another location as the battle progressed.

One day while we were on the move, our convoy pulled off the road for a lunch break. (By this time we had a normal complement of

trucks and other vehicles). While we were seated on the ground, finishing our chow, a plane flew overhead at low altitude and we noticed
the unmistakable Luftwaffe emblem on its fuselage. Before the reality
of that sunk in the plane was on us again, this time spraying our little
encampment with machine gun fire. We took cover as best we could,
mostly under the trucks, in time for a second pass by the plane. Some
of the guys took futile potshots at the plane. No one was hurt, but the
war had come to Division Headquarters!

The campaign was waged during July, probably the hottest month
for Sicily. One of the well-criticized Seventh Army edicts was that, by
army order, we had to wear wool uniforms in that heat, and ties(!). At
this removed date, that sounds incredible, but was true. Sicily was hot
and stifling, but beautiful in a primitive way.

The landscape is very rocky and steep with orchards, vineyards
and grain fields dotting the rock-fence enclosed fields of the lower
areas. Many of the hills were terraced for cultivation. The crops were
grapes, tomatoes, melons, grain and olives. There were also citrus
groves, but they were out of season while we were there. The farm
buildings are combination stone and cement, mostly white, decorated
around the doors and kitchen walls with garlands of onions and gar-
lic hanging to dry.

Towns were usually either situated in the lowest areas or along the
coast, but some were on the very tops of the craggy hilltops, put there
in earlier days as bastions against attack. The dominant feature of
every town, in addition to a few cafes and stores, was the town
church, always resplendent in red, green and gold. The contrast
between the richness of the church and the squalor of the usual town
was palpable.

Transportation for the peasantry was by rickety bus or by the
ubiquitous carts drawn by undersized burros. The carts were decorated in shiny enamel with intricate scrollwork, and were obviously the
source of much pride. The roadside was dotted with religious shrines,
which were invariably decorated with flowers.

There were pictures of Mussolini, the Italian dictator, all over, and
the slogan "Vive Duce" (the word vive expressed as two V's joined
almost as in a W but with the two adjoining arms crossed) written on
almost every wall. We understood that the Mafia was in control here

but never saw any evidence of it. The people were hardworking farmers and artisans.

We were strewn with flowers, fruit and wine whenever we passed into a newly liberated town. Most Sicilians have relatives in the U.S. and we were constantly peppered with questions about them. The Italian-American soldiers, particularly, were bombarded, so much so that, after a while, most of them did not own up to being Italian. It was a good feeling to be greeted as liberators, which was true in succeeding days in Italy, France and elsewhere.

Living on the move for the first time brought into focus the problems of bathing and shaving, washing socks, etc., and finding out what was necessary in the field. Husbanding the cigarette supply was always a concern. The individual rations were supplied with small packs of four cigarettes, obviously not enough to last through the day. These were augmented by packages that reached us from time to time from home and also what could be scrounged or traded for.

The rations were either C or K, the K being a meal packed in a box about the size of a Cracker Jack box which would include a small can of food, a packet of biscuits, cigarettes, some hard candy and a packet of instant coffee, cocoa or lemonade. The C-ration was more substantial, being packed in two cans, one of which included the main edible (meant to be heated); the other, including biscuits, cigarettes, some sheets of toilet paper, etc. There was also an emergency D-ration, which was a concentrated chocolate bar weighing several ounces, three bars being enough, it was said, for a day's nourishment.

A great deal of research went into designing these rations and initially they were kind of satisfactory. After a week or so on K's and C'S, though, one had had enough and they actually were repulsive in some cases—the K corned pork loaf being a prime example. On the other hand, we always had something to eat and, after all, we were in a war.

One of the early lessons came to me on one of these days. One evening we pulled up tired and hungry into a farmyard with orders to sack out for the night. In the failing light I found a satisfactory site at the entrance to a barn. I spread out my shelter half, sprinkled around the anti-insect powder given us, drew my blanket over me and fell fast asleep. The next morning, in the light, I observed to my horror/amusement that I had spent the night on a pile of manure! So much for fastidiousness. I really have not been the same in that department ever since.

Our principal anchor to home was the arrival of mail which, throughout the war, was about as prompt as could be expected. Someone high up had decided early on that the delivery of mail was to be given priority. This person should be thanked. I tried to write something every day, although since most of what I wanted to say was censorable my mail home tended to be short on description. On the other hand, I was fortunate to receive lots of mail, which always provided a welcome break.

We wound up outside of Trapani and made our bivouac in a small villa while the bitter fighting continued on the eastern end of the Island. The 505th, in the first two or three days of the battle had sealed the beachhead from German armored reinforcements. Subsequent to that, we only had minor skirmishes, the scenario usually being that some shots would be fired and thereupon the Italian garrison would surrender, having put up a face-saving token resistance. We would occupy the town and almost immediately proceed to the next.

In our villa outside Trapani, we were engaged with writing up various reports, but it was mostly a time with nothing much to do and we used the time to swim in an irrigation tank at our dusty villa and to take an occasional walk up a steep hill by a switch-back road to the medieval walled town of Erice. This was like entering another world, with its cobblestone streets and alleys. It was a time to relax, reflect and consider what lay ahead.

It was about then that the scandal of the soldier-slapping incident broke and we were drawn up in formation (as were all units on the island) to hear Patton's letter of apology. In retrospect that had to be a tremendous come down for him.

Our first campaign was over.

9

ITALY

Our first campaign was over and, as they say, we were blooded. Even though as a Division we went through Sicily piecemeal, we did in those early hours contribute importantly to the outcome. The most dismal note was the debacle on the second night, the shooting down of portions of the 504th, which led to a change in tactics—no more flying over friendly fleets—which in turn led to other difficulties, as will be seen in Normandy.

The gliders were not used to bring our troops to the battlefield because of the limitations of the available airlift. The British, however, did use gliders at their end of the battle, towed by American C-47's. The results were not good.

When we finally assembled as a Division, we were given a mopping up detail from the center to the western end of the island, so that, for the most part, it was a series of dusty rapid advances against a surrendering army while the severe fighting went on to the east.

Changes were made. Colonel Boyd, our G-3, was transferred to the 325th where he was given command of a battalion. Brigadier General Kierans, the Assistant Division Commander, was flying as an unapproved observer with the 504th; he was on a plane that was shot down and he lost his life. His ultimate replacement was Colonel Gavin from the 505th, who was replaced by Batcheller (who later was replaced by Ekman).

Boyd's job was taken over by Colonel "Rusk" (the only man in this book for whom I'll provide an alias), who, as we soon found out, made life miserable for all of us with his nitpicking ways. Planning got

underway almost immediately after the conclusion of the Sicilian campaign for the next step, the invasion of Italy. This strategic decision, as
well as the others before it, was a victory for the British planners
whose "baby" was continued emphasis on the Mediterranean Theater.

We moved back to Africa, this time in the Karouan area, and then
once again back to Sicily, because the airfields there were closer to
Italy. We also embarked on a continuing series of changing plans for
the upcoming invasion. With each new plan we (in G-3) had to develop the schemes that covered entry planning, loads and various aircraft
serials, mapping, tentative field orders, and the like. With the plan
constantly changing, and Rusk altering the alterations, we literally
worked day and night. A building was eventually commandeered for
our use in the town of Comiso and some nights we did our work there.

Working for the Captain-Queeg-like Colonel Rusk was quite
unpleasant, particularly after having been under the command of
Colonel Boyd. Rusk was possibly insecure and his solution to all problems was overkill, wreaking his worst on officers and men alike. Many
were the days we literally worked around the clock doing and re-doing
various schemes and plans, seeking the perfection demanded by our
obsessed leader. Mehrholz took most of the brunt of Rusk's nonsense
as it related to all of us. We were an unhappy ship. Rusk was a jittery,
nervous guy and belied his southern roots by acting more like a fast-
talking northerner (southern accent and all). He was a confusing picture. He had this silver Eversharp pencil, one that accommodated individual lengths of lead, and he was constantly misplacing it. At the cry,
"Anybody seen my mechanical pencil?" all work would cease until the
pencil was found.

Once, before we started using the indoor night facility in Comiso,
we were outside and spread out under some trees alongside our field
tent which had the sides rolled up—altogether an area some 20 or 25
feet square. This is hard to believe, even as I write many years later.
We were working at night and the pencil once again became the subject of a hunt. This time, when the pencil was not found, Rusk had a
couple of jeeps brought up, had their headlights trained on the area,
and he forced us to cross and recross the area we were working in,
eyes down, in search of his blankety-blank pencil! It was not found.
Secretly, I think we were all happy with that outcome.

The next morning, after a few hours sleep, we had some breakfast and Sgt. Mehrholz came up to me and quietly said, "Let's take a walk." He had been under a much greater strain than the rest of us and I assumed he wanted to unburden himself to someone in private. We walked a few hundred yards from where our G-3 tent was set up— going up a wooded hill overlooking a deep ravine. We had been talking about the number one subject—that miserable SOB Colonel of ours—when Bill stopped, looked around to make sure we were not observed, reached into his pocket and, with a small smile of triumph, took out the mechanical pencil! He hefted it a couple of times in his right hand, exclaimed "May he rot in hell!" (he rarely swore) and then reached back and hurled that pencil as far as he could. We watched it tumbling in the air as it slowly descended into the ravine. Bill had had his revenge.

A moment of irony occurred years later in the 1990s when the deaths of both Mehrholz and Rusk were noted in the same issue of the Division Association's Quarterly—the *Paraglide*.

And then came the blockbuster—Operation Giant. A hurried meeting was called of the regimental and artillery commanders and key staff (I was there, pencil and paper in hand in case I was needed, by order of Colonel Rusk). The plan was unfolded by a grim General Ridgway. The Mediterranean Command (Eisenhower) had been in contact with the Italian government led by Badoglio, developing an astounding scenario. General Maxwell Taylor, the 82d Assistant Division Commander (soon to be given command of the 101st Airborne Division), would go under the cover of night to the Italian coast near Rome and be picked up and spirited into the capital where he would confer with the Italian high command. The plan was for the Italians to clear the way for our Division to jump and otherwise land on Rome's airfields, whereupon the Italian Army would join with us to defend the city from German attack. At the same time, a landing would be made in the Salerno area by our seaborne Fifth Army under General Mark Clark. If Taylor's mission made a positive appraisal of the proposed arrangement, he would so signal by wireless to Eisenhower and Ridgway and the airborne mission would be on!

This was the stuff that movies are made of. When the meeting ended (with my services not having been needed), I rushed back to our tent where I sat on a five gallon can of water and recorded what I had just heard on a scrap of paper which I have to this day.

And so a new plan was made, with us working around the clock to produce it. Rations and ammunition were issued, briefings were held and the planes loaded, with H-Hour rapidly approaching. Similarly, the seaborne force for the invasion of the Salerno beaches was approaching its destination and would land the following morning. Everything was in readiness awaiting the message from General Taylor. It is said that some of our planes were already in the air—certainly motors were turning over on the airfields—when word came that the mission was off.

Years later it became known that Ridgway was opposed to Giant because he felt it would be suicidal. What the planning also did was prevent us from being in on the initial assault at Salerno. In the event, the sea invasion was made, there were immediate difficulties on land, and the 505th and 504th were hurriedly flown to the battlefield and dropped within our lines. The rest of the Division followed; my route was by C-47, which landed on a hastily carved landing strip near the Salerno beach. The invasion of Italy, code-named Avalanche, went in on the Salerno beaches by the newly constituted Fifth Army.

Seventh Army, the force in Sicily, was basically disbanded, a good part of it being sent to England to serve as a veteran nucleus for the army that would invade France. These units included the First and Ninth Infantry Divisions, the Second Armored Division and, later on, us—the 82d Airborne Division. Seventh Army remained as a headquarters group until being re-constituted for the invasion into Southern France in the summer of 1944.

Patton was suffering from the semi-disgrace of his dismissal following the soldier-slapping incidents and was off to England. In later years I queried Jack Norton, who retired from the Army as a Lt. General, and was Operations Officer of the 505th at the time of the incidents, asking what, if any, is the current position of the Army on the affair—how is it taught at West Point, for example? Whether relieving him of his command meant that, in 1944, Bradley not Patton would command the American troops entering France. Norton said unequivocally that the punishment was not too severe, and that what Patton had done was inexcusable.

Contrary to the esteem with which he was later held in Europe as commander of the Third Army, his reputation post-Sicily was as low as it could get among men who had served under him in the Seventh Army. Coincidentally or otherwise, those major units that served under Patton in the Mediterranean never were part of his command in Europe. (This is a pet theory of mine—I suspect that the apology was the reason.)

The Avalanche plan was to invade by sea at Salerno, be joined in the course of the battle by the British Eighth Army, which would make a concurrent landing at the southeastern end of Italy and fight their way northward, joining up with the American Fifth Army as soon as possible, then marching side by side to the north with the city of Naples as the immediate target.

The invasion was made in early September and the inexperienced Americans, none of the divisions having seen action before, ran into deep trouble on the beachhead. A hurry-up call was sent to us, still being in a state of preparedness on airfields in Sicily and Africa, and the 82d made a series of parachute drops on the beachhead and immediately went to the aid of the beleaguered 5th Army troops. A group of us from Headquarters was air-landed in C-47's on airstrips, which were hastily set up on the shore.

As we moved northward, our route took us along the Amalfi Drive, which is the spectacular southern side of the Sorrento Peninsula. It was gorgeous, but a hell of a place to fight a war because the steep mountains and deep gorges were perfect for defense. But the Germans apparently planned to make their defensive line further north. They withdrew slowly and grudgingly, but withdraw they did.

I remember coming into the seacoast town of Maori, where some of our troops had come in on naval landing craft. Maori was at the base of a mountain system rising from the sea which led to the Chiunzi Pass, the other side of which led down to the plains below the city of Naples, which was a major objective of ours. Some of our troops and also some Rangers under the command of the legendary Colonel Darby were dug in at the summit near the pass and on the flanks of the mountain below. Townspeople were used as bearers of cartons of foods and ammunition to the troops on the mountain. At that point, the usual great advantage of our army—its motor transport—had not caught up with the advance elements. These residents were paid with food which had been brought in by landing craft from naval sources. A minor riot broke out in Maori when the rations were being distributed, momentarily becoming a greater problem than the battle with the enemy. It was disturbing but settled after a few hours.

At the top of the mountain, which was reached by a lightly traveled and poorly graded dirt road, there were a couple of small buildings. The men near these buildings had dug holes not downward into the ground but sideways into the near vertical sides of the mountain, something I never saw before nor since. Ridgway had established an advance CP here and I was part of it. It was a mixed-up force that included some of our men, Rangers and some British liaison people.

An advance was to be made during the night with the Rangers and paratroopers going down the side of the mountain toward Naples in quiet—no artillery preparation—and with jeeps that would follow moving down the slopes without using their engines. I remember being impressed with the purposefulness of the Rangers and the calm demeanor of their leader, Colonel Darby. In the event, the advance went off without a hitch and by daylight we were in possession of both sides of the mountain and the way to Naples was open before us.

We stayed one night in a town, Torre Annunziata, in preparation for the advance into Naples. Some motor transport and rations caught up with us. Again there was another riotous Italian scene with the volatile populace celebrating, denouncing the local Fascist leadership and wreaking physical vengeance on them. Not having police troops with us, and with bigger things on the fire, we had more or less to let those things happen without intervention or attempts to establish some sort of justice system. That came later when the AMGOT specialists arrived.

Naples fell to us with only light skirmishing along the way. We were greeted on our triumphant entry by wildly cheering, emotional crowds of Italians. We really felt like conquering heroes. But my first job was to scrounge around the neighborhood in an unsuccessful attempt to get hold of some candles. We established ourselves in the Questura (police headquarters) from which base we carried out some activities north on the Volturno River, but in a piecemeal manner. The division was slated to go to England to become part of the 1944 cross-

Channel force, and it was only a matter of time before we were to be completely relieved.

Naples was something else. It was a large city built on a crescent rising from the waterfront. From the sea it must have a fantastic appearance, rising as it does in white and pastel colors to the apex of the steep hills. On the ground it is another matter, because much of the city is a warren of alleys with stairways in some cases in place of streets. There was no vegetation—all was stone and cement. We were at sea level in the Questura, which was located on a major square with a large cobble-stoned open area surrounded by government buildings including the post office, which was located across the square, maybe 300 feet from where we were. From the square, the major street, the via Roma, led to the waterfront. At or near the waterfront were the royal palace and a large museum, which were both closed tight. Along the waterfront and for one or two streets parallel to it were bars and brothels, which have served seafaring people for centuries. Along the via Roma there was a large open gallery of fine shops which kept doors open even during the period when the war raged around them.

All electric power, which was controlled from the north, had been cut off by the retreating Germans, so the city was in the dark. After a couple of days, as if the oversight was recognized, the water supply, also from the north, was cut off and then the city was without water, a much more serious situation. There were some wells lining the waterfront, and all day long a stream of the populace headed toward these spigots, carrying empty bottles and pots, to stand in line waiting their turn. They then headed back up the hills toward their homes with the precious water. This went on for months.

We attempted to fill up our water-carrying trucks, establish a spot away from the shore and distribute water to whoever showed up, but this too, as with the rations in Maori, caused riots among the civilians and we had to give up the idea.

The port of Naples, which was needed desperately for supplies, had been rendered non-usable by the Germans, as they sunk ships, mined channels, and blew up the docks, so that it took weeks before the port was in use by our Navy. The apple-cheeked sailors, having access to terra firma, were a source of amusement as none of them, it seemed, when they got a day's leave from their ship, managed to get beyond the immediate waterfront. As with centuries of their forbears, they found (or lost) themselves in the fleshpots right near the shore.

At some point, the Germans embarked on a campaign of night bombing of the city, which did not do too much damage but was a nuisance. As it happened, by that time I was no longer in Naples.

There was one startling event, however. The post office building across the square from us was being used by some troops (not 82d men) when, suddenly, at mid-day when men were having chow, there was a tremendous explosion. At the time I happened to be leaning out of the Questura's second floor window talking with someone on the street below, and felt the great sucking-in of air followed by an outward rush of air and noise coming from the bombed building. Heavy explosives had been left by the Germans, who assumed the building would be used by our troops, and they had set delayed timers. There were many deaths and everybody rushed over and pitched in to dig out the grisly remains.

But fortunately, I was to leave Naples shortly.

10

ONCE MORE ON THE OCEAN

While we were in action up to Naples, associations with Colonel Rusk became a little less onerous. But when we got to that city the usual "chicken shit" started up again. So when I heard I was to be leaving Naples for a special assignment, I was overjoyed. There was to be some testing of new equipment for Pathfinding. A group of about 20 men from the 505th, headed by Captain Jack Norton, then either a company commander or Regimental S-3, were going back to an airfield at Comiso in Sicily where this equipment, chaperoned by some of its sponsors in Washington, would be tested. I was going because they needed someone to make sketches, keep a diary and produce the final report of the project, which would be authored by Jack Norton.

Pathfinding was the technique whereby highly trained specialists would be dropped in advance of a main body of paratrooprs with the mission of locating the drop zones to be used by the following men, marking them with panels, smoke devices and/or radio beacons. The testing to be done involved the use of radar devices. With the night landings in Europe on the horizon, needless to say the testing was of major importance.

We were billeted in a barracks at the Comiso airfield, which was also being used by some of the Division's rear echelon. It is unfair to tar a whole group with the same brush but, in the main, rear echelons were made up to some extent of personnel who were not wanted for other assignments. There were obviously some guys doing drugs, because the first time I left my things in the barracks, the parachute first aid kit, which included morphine, was stolen from my bag.

73

This was my first meeting with Jack Norton, who later became G-3 of the Division. Norton was a young West Point-trained captain in his twenties. Tall and well spoken, with an open face and broad brow and booming (at times) voice, he approached the business of war with a seriousness and professionalism I had not observed before from close up. In those early days at Comiso and later on, when he took over as Division G-3 after Normandy, I never saw him angry or without the good cheer and ability to cut to the essence of the matter at hand. These were his hallmarks and gained him the respect of all he worked with. After the days with Durwood Rusk, this assignment was akin to heaven. I didn't have too much to do except type up daily reports, which I usually accompanied with some sketches. The final report took about two days and all went smoothly. Many years later I found out Norton had been Cadet Captain at West Point. Also, to my amazement, in view of the importance of his duties, I found that he was the same age as I. Truly, one of the "Heroes."

At this point there were rear echelon groups all over Sicily (also some in North Africa). The plan was to evacuate North Africa, Sicily and Italy of 82d troops and they would all meet in the harbor at Oran (Mers El Kebir) sometime in mid to late November 1943, from which point they would go by convoy to England. It developed that there was some very high-level struggling going on about this as General Clark (Fifth Army), together with the "soft underbelly" British group didn't want to let us go. In the event, one third of the Division, the 504th Regimental Combat Team, was left behind. They fought starting in January at Anzio and finally came to England just before the June 1944 invasion, too late for them to participate.

However, my special Sicily assignment was extended because someone was needed to collect passenger lists of the ships as they were loaded with our men and then take these passenger lists to Naples. And I was nominated. Some groups would be loaded at Augusta, some at Siracusa, and there may have been other departure points as well. I was given a schedule, a jeep and a corporal who I didn't know to accompany me. This man was chosen because he was Italian-American and spoke the language fluently. I have forgotten his name.

I had written orders that gave me carte blanche to ask for food, fuel and lodging, and we were on our own. It worked and we collected the lists on schedule, solemnly saluting as the various LCI's pushed away from the wharves. I had to report to British Naval Offices in Siracusa and Augusta and I believe they were amused by me and my lack of heel-stamp saluting when reporting at an official installation. Anyway, we made the rounds and then had to leave the island of Sicily.

Somehow we wound up in Bari, which is on the eastern end of the tip of Italy. It wasn't as easy to cadge off the British as our own army (particularly when it came to gas for the jeep), but I was persuasive enough. British Army food was less both in quantity and quality to ours, but my "interpreter" was always able to procure something from the locals due to his use of the language.

The night we stayed over in Bari we went to a movie theater where they were showing an Edward G. Robinson movie dubbed into Italian. It was super funny because in the film Robinson finds himself among some British upper class and the varying interpretations of Robinson-ese and British upper-class speak as they were rendered in Italian were hilarious. There was also Italian vaudeville as performed by warring claques in the audience. Somehow, this evening in the theater remains with me as the clearest image of the trip from Sicily back to Naples.

On returning to Naples and rejoining the group, still at the Questura, there was shocking news. Mehrholz had been busted by Colonel Rusk and sent back to the 80th Anti-Aircraft Battalion (where he had started). Rusk had ridden him mercilessly in the days up to his demotion and, in his place, Rusk had brought Dorant back from the 325th Glider Infantry, promoting him once again to Master Sergeant and head of section.

This was, besides being unfair to poor, humiliated Mehrholz, who had done his job well, a blow to both me and Graddy Richard, who were being passed over in favor of Dorant. Richard said nothing and neither did I, but of course we were both chagrined. This had little to do with Dorant. I liked Chester and we had always gotten along well and would continue to do so in the future. He was a decent guy. It was just an example of the frustrations that came with being in the service, as many millions have found out.

Complicating all this was a set-to I had with the Colonel a day or two after I came back from Sicily. We had a map that covered the Italian front in relatively small scale and we would routinely update the positions of the various divisions on the map based on Situation Reports we received from Fifth Army and other headquarters. Rusk was viewing the map with a visitor and called me to task, expressing his view that the postings were incorrect. I dug out the written material from which the map was posted and he didn't like the way I pointed out the data to him. After a few exchanges, he directed me to "observe the courtesies of the service," thus reminding me of the differences in our positions, and then dismissed me from the area. Actually, this coming as close as it did to the Mehrholz affair found me acting resentfully and fairly heedless of the consequences—of which I was sure there would be some.

While I was contemplating the possibilities in the ensuing days— none came immediately—in its place came rescue from an unexpected source: Colonel Lynch, our G-2, had been sent to the 36th Infantry Division to take over one of their regiments and (glory be) Rusk was assigned as our G-2, in turn replaced as G-3 by Colonel Turner, who came out of our 325th. While this was bad news for Jim Spotswood and his G-2 crew, we were overjoyed and I was off the hook. Whew!

Somewhere in the middle of all this, I was surprised and pleased to receive a Letter of Commendation from Jack Norton relating to my services to the Pathfinder program at Comiso. It was addressed to the Commanding General, 82d Division, and was made part of my official record. It was something of a morale builder after the recent events.

It was time to take stock. By now I had been in the Army for about a year. The early heady days when I was promoted quickly were past. I had hoped to get the opportunity to go to Officers Candidate School but the opportunity never presented itself—first, things were frozen because we were slated to go overseas; once there, we were in a war zone and, again, the opportunity never knocked. I had satisfied myself that I could do what was required of me and, generally speaking, I was a good soldier. However, there were dead-end aspects to my position for which I had no answer. On the plus side, I had plenty of company in my disappointments, deriving comfort from living the shared trials of our little G-3 band.

I had proven I could handle my job and was pleased that I had been selected to go on the Pathfinding trial program. I was trusted enough to pick up those passenger lists and get them back to Naples, with responsibility for details left to me. It was a heady experience to be on my own, if only for a short period of time during which I made my own decisions and was free to organize my own schedule. It was fun. But back to reality. Our few remaining days in Naples passed quickly. The Division, except for the 504th, was extracted from contact with the enemy and we packed our stuff and marched in full regalia to the waterfront in the now bustling port and loaded onto the USS *Frederick Funston*, a Navy transport which would be our home for the next month or so. We were off!

There was an elaborate ceremonial saber and scabbard which I had liberated from the walls of the Questura and was intent on taking with me. Unfortunately, its length was such that I couldn't completely cover it with my rolled up shelter half and blanket, which in turn was part of my backpack—in fact, the handle stuck out. I thought I could get away with it, fearing that if I put it in one of my barracks bags, which would be transported and loaded onto the ship separate from our persons, it would be "re-liberated" by whoever might see it sticking out of one of the bags. I was nailed, however, on the wharf. Captain Chandler of Headquarters Company saw the handle sticking out and ordered me to divest myself. He was OK about it though, just pointing out in an exaggerated formal voice that "the dismounted soldier does not carry a saber." I hurriedly placed it in one of my bags, which was among those piled up prior to being thrown on trucks, and returned to the ranks. That, of course, was the last I saw of the sword. Ah, me.

Our first step was the aforementioned marshalling of the convoy off the North African coast at Oran. Actually, Oran was separated from the sea by some hills and its port was Mers El Kebir, connected to Oran by tunneling through the hills. There we settled at sea for a few days, giving us the chance to get cleaned up and get our clothes, mail and other items in order. We had a memorable Thanksgiving dinner anchored at sea off MEK.

It was our third experience at sea on an oceangoing ship. We learned that in the Navy the word "boat" referred to something about the size of a rowboat and it was never used in regard to anything larger. The first was on the *Washington*, the converted liner we crossed the ocean in. That was a merchant ship, clumsily converted to transport duty and was very crowded and uncomfortable. I had had the good luck as described earlier to have a green armband and the run of the ship, avoiding what all the other guys had to endure. The *Monrovia*, which was the command ship going into Sicily, also had its limitations, being swollen with passengers and quite crowded. The *Funston*, in contrast, was designed as a Navy troop ship and was comparatively comfortable, though with plain pipe rack accommodations. The food was great and there were three meals per day. The Navy took great care in keeping everything squeaky clean.

The assembling convoy was scattered about offshore—not at docks. Some of the ships were possibly a mile out. "Liberty" (that good naval term) parties were set up and we all had turns spending a day in Oran. We were picked up by an LCVP, which circled throughout the ships at anchor and deposited us at the wharf, which was a concrete roadway several feet above the level of the sea. Trucks transported us through the mountains into Oran, dropped us off, and we were cautioned not to miss the last truck to leave the central point for the wharf.

The day consisted of walking around, having coffee and doughnuts at the Red Cross—seemingly not too much, but it was free and safe which was the big point of it. I don't remember at this time who I was with, but we made our way back as directed and boarded an LCVP in the darkness and settled onto one of the few metal benches, ready for the moonlit trip through the gentle waves back to the *Funston*. We had pushed away and were heading about to the open harbor, when we were abruptly summoned back by a Shore Patrol jeep, which screeched to a halt just above us.

"We have one more for you," and the SP's hauled an inert body from the back of their jeep, staggered to the edge of the concrete with it and unceremoniously dumped the obviously passed out sailor into the LCVP, he landing with a loud clang.

The guy just laid there like a sack of grain as we circled away from the wharf and headed out to the harbor with him lying there. Now, aboard our craft were a couple of those apple-cheeked seamen (who never failed to amaze us grizzled soldiers with their youth and innocence). One of them sidled over to the inert form, studied him and then shouted to his buddy, "Why, it's that drunken son-of-a-bitch Mabius, ha, ha, ha!"

His buddy came over and the two of them practically did a war dance over the body, chortling and repeating, "It's that drunken SOB, Mabius, ha, ha, ha!" By now, we are all intrigued and noticed that the drunk was wearing the insignia of a Boatswain's Mate, which is the equivalent of a First Sergeant, and arrived at the conclusion that this Mabius, when sober, was the bane of these poor seamens' existence. We were all duly entertained by the sight of the inert body and the hysterically celebrating sailors.

Suddenly, the "corpse" stirred and struggled to his feet, bellowing, "Who called me a drunken son-of-a-bitch?" He kept repeating that as he grew more awake and sober and finally zeroed in on those two poor kids who were now practically trembling and looking for nonexistent places to hide. One of them started pleading, "I wouldn't call you an SOB—if I did, then I am an SOB and I wouldn't call myself an SOB, now, would I, Mabius?" This went on for a while and Mabius kept getting more and more enraged and the two sailors more and more terrified. It looked like Mabius was getting ready to throw them overboard, one by one.

Cooler heads among the soldiers intervened, cordoning off the two kids from Mabius and heaven knows what happened when they finally got to their ship. For us who witnessed it, it was one of the funniest things ever and it is one of the events that is as clear to me now as it was the many years ago when it happened. Literally thousands of times I have marveled at the miraculous recovery and rebound of CPO Mabius. And even now I smile at the recollection, somehow the funniest part being the repetition of the name "Mabius," which has a great sound to it.

It came to pass that in late November 1943, some days after that scrumptious Thanksgiving dinner, we were off to the north, to the British Isles and our ultimate mission, the invasion of France. Now we knew that we would undoubtedly be in on that from the start—nothing would happen during the coming winter and we knew that we and some other divisions were being sent from the Mediterranean to furnish an experienced core to the invading army for the awesome event which we knew finally had to come in 1944.

But at the time we were still at sea in the placid Mediterranean, headed for the Strait of Gibraltar with all its dangers. After that we would be in the open ocean, en route for England. In the event, despite all the trepidation, the convoy slipped through during the night without incident, past Gibraltar and into the broad Atlantic. Our course was to take us straight out almost to mid-ocean to miss the sub-infested waters off France, then turn north, and ultimately east. For some reason our destination was changed to Northern Ireland and we landed in Belfast after about 20 days at sea.

The trip was uneventful and, ultimately, boring. During the voyage Jim Spotswood of G-2 and I spent a lot of time together and we established a firm friendship that lasted throughout the war. Jim was from Mississippi and a newspaperman before entering the service. Along with me, he was one of the few guys who were married. He was tall, thin and spoke very quietly and sparingly. He was absolutely on the level and we formed that unusual alliance of the tall, quiet Southerner and the short, fast-talking Jewish New Yorker.

We spent hours, it seemed, on deck, at the rail ruminating about the war, life, literature, good and bad officers and everything else. We talked politics. These many years later the words "anti-fascism" and "social justice" have an unrealistic ring but they were my credo. Jim had inherited Colonel Rusk from us, and, as a friend, I filled him in on what I knew of Rusk. Jim, who held the rank of Master Sergeant, was Chief of Section, G-2, on the same level held by Dorant in G-3.

There was, of course, no incoming mail, but I wrote a long letter during the voyage, adding something each day. We were obviously proscribed in what we could write, so composing the letter was somewhat frustrating. On the other hand, I was anxiously awaiting some news about becoming a father, which was on an any-day basis. There was a lot of unreality in the contrasts involved, being at war, being at sea, and anxiously awaiting news from home.

Some of us established a pinochle game, which was played on the steel plate deck of our sleeping compartment, in poor light and with rapidly deteriorating decks of cards. We played for pennies and, since we didn't have any currency, kept a running score. At the end, I was ahead over $240 which was quite a lot for a penny game and it was all settled when we finally received our pay in Ireland. If I had been losing in the game, I would have left it at some point because it was becoming boring, but as the winner I was obliged to continue. It eventually became a chore, but better than no activity at all.

We became accustomed to the Navy routine, the watches, the public address announcements about when smoking was permitted—"The smoking lamp is lit"—practices of "General Quarters," in which everybody had a station, the sailors to weapons, etc., and we to assemble on the deck with life jackets on. "Charley Noble is smoking" meant that the galley was spewing out smoke (a no-no). "Sweepers man your brooms. Clean sweep down fore and aft," was just what it said and happened every day. Each announcement was preceded by "Now hear this." There were three watches and each one took normal four-hour turns, two each day, except in the event of a special assignment or emergency. There were life raft drills and other things of that nature, all called into action over the public address system. If the event called for action like manning battle stations, but was a drill only, it would be followed by the words, "This is a drill."

One day we were being lectured to below decks in an open area near our bunks by Lieutenant Bankston. Now, from time to time there would be someone eminently unqualified to hold the position he had and such was Bankston. Practically illiterate, with vocabulary to match, he was giving us some required lecture, possibly on the Articles of War, much to our eye-rolling disgust and amusement at his mislocutions and verbal boo-boos. Then, over the public address came the attention-grabbing announcement, "General Quarters, General Quarters, all hands General Quarters. This is no drill!" At this, Bankston froze for what seemed to be minutes, teetered on his feet and, with ashen face, swallowed and repeated "This is no drill," and stumbled out of the area leaving us to our own devices. We hastened to don our life jackets and proceed outside to the deck which was our position during General Quarters. We were soon falling over each other laughing when the order was rescinded. We never knew why the call had been sounded, but we never got over the sight of poor Bankston "under fire," and it caused much entertainment for us in the days to come. The utterance of "This is no drill," was always good for a laugh from those of us who had attended that long forgotten lecture.

The journey was ending, thankfully uneventfully, and we were coming into the harbor at Belfast under gray skies and low, fast-moving clouds. Later on, through my readings about the war, and particularly the Battle of the Atlantic, I discovered that, by the Fall of 1943, the battle had been tipped in our favor through the use of sonar, radar, increased radius of some aircraft and the overall tactics developed by the English, Canadian and American navies.

In Northern Ireland we were handed a welcome pamphlet with a picture of and message from Winston Churchill, prepared our packs and barracks bags and were off to the next adventure!

11

IRELAND

We eagerly surveyed the scene from the deck before disembarking on that dark late morning. The most striking aspect of the low brick buildings bordering the waterfront were all the chimneys, most of them with a curl of dark smoke blending into the atmosphere. We were to learn to our amazement that the main source of heat throughout the British Isles was, in the main, an open soft coal burning fireplace, each with its own chimney and located one to a room. There were also some gas heaters, with the gas being metered out a shilling's-worth at a time.

We were to rapidly get used to the pound, shilling, pence system and the bulky coins. But on this day, we drank in the atmosphere. The buildings and houses looked squat, grimy and discolored, most probably through exposure all those years to coal smoke. And we were delighted at the prospect of being in an English speaking country, although there were the clashes of accents that led to many a frustrating encounter.

Then we were trucked to Castle Dawson, a town some 30 or so miles south of Belfast, near the border with the Free State of Ireland which was neutral in the war, choosing not to join with its bitter enemy, Great Britain. One would think that this would cause some difficulties, but no, having Ireland just miles away from where we were stationed didn't cause any problems. Irish revolutionary songs were sung by the locals in the romantic atmosphere of the smoke-filled pubs, but there were no overt problems between us and the many sympathizers of the Irish Republican Army to whom we were exposed. It was obvious that the hatred toward the English was not passed on and directed toward us.

The camp we were billeted at consisted of rows of corrugated metal buildings called Nissan or Quonset huts, some of which were used for our headquarters and the others for living quarters. The barracks were furnished with hard cots, on which we placed mattress covers, which we stuffed with straw, the resulting piece being called a tick. Not the most comfortable arrangement, but we got used to it.

We also got used to the short days, it being December with winter at hand. It didn't get light until after 9 AM and by 3 PM darkness was closing in. Each morning we had Reveille when we lined up in the dark on a road parallel to our row of huts, but somewhat below it. On the other side of this narrow road there was another drop-off into a wooded ravine. The formation was conducted in pitch-blackness with no light being permitted because we were under blackout conditions. So we had this long lineup of men, with the ravine to their backs, seen as a mass of shadowy figures under clouds of steamy breath. It didn't take too many days for most of the guys to realize that, with vision as bad as it was, one could shuffle out to the formation clothed only in shoes and overcoat, thus gaining a few minutes extra sleep. The next step was that instead of facing front (the embankment on which the huts were located), one could face to the rear and urinate into the ravine as the roll was called. This despoiling of the environment was the source of much laughter and satisfaction.

In spite of the short periods of daylight, the landscape was a rich, dark green all over—mainly due, we were told, to the frequent and steady rainfall which occurred throughout the year. The Emerald Isle! The Division settled rapidly into an accelerated training schedule and we were quite busy in G-3 keeping up with all the activity. We were also acclimatizing ourselves to our new chief, Colonel Turner, who we rapidly found to be a fine officer.

Some words are in order about our officers. Colonel Boyd had been a pleasure to serve with, as was his assistant, Captain Leahy. They both went on to be battalion commanders, and later on Boyd became part of the staff of the Allied Airborne Army when it was formed in 1944.

Two officers who served with us in G-3 for most of the war were

Captains Gerard and Marston. Richard Gerard was from Lake Charles, La., and was a lawyer in civilian life. He was very amiable and a guy any of us could talk to when confronted with a problem. He had a feel for the men and seemingly enjoyed talking with us from time to time. He became assistant to Norton later on, and even later became a battalion commander in the 325th Glider Infantry in the Battle of the Bulge. He was also, to our dismay, a friend to his fellow Louisianan, Durwood Rusk.

Hunter Marston III was a Social Register New Yorker with an artillery background. He was with us through all our campaigns. Tall and reticent, his somewhat bashful smile broadcast his sunny nature. He was also someone we could talk with. The group of officers we had in Ireland—Turner, Gerard and Marston—made life once again pleasant within our little G-3 Section.

A couple of days after our arrival in Ireland there was a bonanza of mail. I sorted out the pile of letters, written one per day from Alice, and read them in order, being kept up to date on the impending miracle of birth, which still had not happened. This caused a little embarrassment, because we had been sealed in Fort Bragg from mid-March 1943, and the 9-month gestation period from that date had passed. However, the last visit I made to New York, on a forged 3-day pass, had been in early April, just before we left Fort Bragg. Anyway, still no birth but it was marvelous getting all that mail, and some packages containing goodies as well.

One of the things that happened was the opening up of applications for Officer's Candidate School, the first time that was available to me in the 15 months I was in the Army. I filled in mine as soon as I could, as did Graddy Richard, who was applying for the Judge Advocate's School. We each approached Capt. Gerard of our section, asking him for a necessary Letter of Recommendation, which he graciously agreed to give. We turned our applications in with accompanying letters (including in my case the Letter of Commendation from Norton) and other material, and awaited the convening of the board, which would meet, interview the applicants and make decisions as to who would be recommended for OCS. The Board was headed by Colonel Barrett, who was the Division Inspector General. But before Barrett could do anything, he was taken ill and all action was postponed until his recovery and return to duty. Once again, chagrin at one more roadblock on the way to OCS.

What was also afoot were furloughs, which would be of 10-day duration and could be taken almost anywhere within England, Northern Ireland and Scotland. I was one of the first to go and I naturally chose London as my destination. Oddly enough, I was about the only one in the initial group who picked London. I made the trip with written reservations in the Hans Crescent Hotel in Knightsbridge. (I loved the sound of those British names.) I also had train tickets, a ration card and a series of pamphlets on how to behave.

First, a train trip to Belfast, which left us close to the dock from which the ferry to Scotland would leave. I was soon to find out about the Irish Sea in December and why this crossing is described as one of the world's worst. The ferry was a stubby tug-like boat and when its engines were throbbing you knew you were aboard a powerful vessel. We steamed out of the relatively placid harbor and onto the open sea, plunging and shuddering into the cold waves, which sent mountains of spray over the decks. The inside cabin included a snack bar which was so inviting while we were still in the harbor. Now the sight and odor of food were nauseating. Most of the passengers took on a sickly shade of yellow-green, and first the lavatory, then the cabin became full of retching passengers, the floors sloppy with vomit and with the atmosphere a sickening odor. I remembered the advice I had been given on the Atlantic crossing and which I had used in a similar situation on the way to Sicily. That was to go out on deck, brace yourself well and fix your glance on the horizon. In that fashion I rode out the waves and arrived in Stranrear in Scotland as one of the few who had not succumbed to mal-de-mer.

Then onto the train to London. This was not a troop train but regular service of the first-rate English rail system. I stayed up all night (to this day I have never been able to sleep on a train) anticipating my coming adventure in the city of Shakespeare and Dickens and the Blitz.

Compared to our rail system, England's was a marvel. Powered by small, sleek coal engines, the trains were comfortable, the road-bed smooth, and they ran on time! After an overnight trip, we slipped into Kings Cross-St. Pancras Station in the northern part of London. I rarely had been so excited because I was here as a sightseer with upwards of a week to "do" the city. Since I had only one week's vacation in all the time I had worked from 1933 to 1942, and my travels in the States had only been a couple of overnights to Philadelphia and Washington, I was ready for this adventure. The only real vacation I had had since I started working was the one unforgettable week Alice and I had spent in Colebrook, Connecticut, just before I reported for duty in the Fall of 1942.

London was worn at the edges but somehow very vital. People moved about purposefully, even though, on close examination, their worn clothes showed the results of constant repair and patching. Having withstood the rigors of the air bombardment for many years, they were not defeated; in fact, they were indomitable, carrying on with pride.

We got to the hotel (I don't remember whether by army transportation or by taxi) and found it to be a modest brick building named after the semi-circular road on which it was located. It consisted of a downstairs reception area, a small dining room and an equally small lounge. This lounge featured large photographs of Roosevelt, Stalin, Churchill and deGaulle on the paneled walls, giving the lounge a United Nations atmosphere. On its (as I remember) four floors, there were about thirty rooms. I was given a room which I shared with another soldier who I hardly ever saw. Breakfast and supper were served in this Red Cross-operated hotel. Lunch was on our own and it developed that I ate most of my dinners out. The hotel was located across the street from the large London department store, Harrod's, and a couple of blocks from Knightsbridge. Kensington and Hyde Park were nearby. The Underground (subway) was located a couple of blocks away and (as with the railroads) they were very well run and easy to get around once you learned the transfer points between the various lines.

By the time I had settled in and taken a brief walk around the immediate neighborhood, it was getting dark and I went back to the hotel for dinner and then into the blackout for a longer walk which took me to the main streets and back. I was fascinated by the bustling figures in the complete darkness, the shafts of light that would flash when a door was opened and closed, and the knowledge that I was, indeed, in London. I stepped into a bar and ordered a beer and was startled to observe a well dressed woman, with a small dog, stride up to the bar and order a double gin! (In this BBC voice, no less.) This at a time when at home no woman would walk into a bar alone and, perish forbid, order a drink. But this was the custom, whether brought about by the war or not I didn't know.

On the way back to the hotel, I switched on my flashlight a couple of times to get my bearings and was gently admonished by a Bobby that I should avoid doing that because of the blackout. I came to discover that all windows had double opaque curtains, and doorways had inner and outer components—so that the door behind was closed before the one ahead was opened, thereby preserving the darkness. Everybody complied with the regulations as a matter of course and we did too as soon as we learned the drill.

I spent a good part of my time just walking around. The Blitz was at a low ebb in December of 1943 and the streets were clear of rubble. Many buildings were destroyed and almost all had at least some damage, but the streets bustled with activity and the usable parts of the damaged buildings were in service. The worst damage was to the East End of London along the Thames River where the bombs had been meant for the nearby port. Block after block was flattened, with the rubble being pushed back from the streets and piled up on the building sites where, in many cases, foliage had taken over. Everyone acknowledged that one of the first post-war jobs would be the rebuilding of the bombed-out areas.

I did the Abbey, the Cathedral, walked the streets of the City of London, the Tower Bridge, Houses of Parliament (not open to the public), the Circuses (squares or plazas to us) and just observed, reaching the conclusion fairly quickly that London reminded me of New York. In fact, the London of all the various regional accents was easiest to understand for me and, as I found out, other GI's from New York. I went to the movies, almost all the films being American.

I made friends at a bookshop with a married couple who went out of their way to make my visit memorable. Harold Goldman was a journalist who worked for a small magazine and had not been accepted for service because of a severely atrophied leg. His wife, Mabel, was a frail woman who was shortly to become pregnant, at which time she left London. They opened their flat to me and saw to it that I met other people, inviting me to a number of small evening parties, which were short on food but long on beer and good fellowship. My proximity to Harrod's on two different occasions permitted me to follow the crowd into the store when it developed that some gin was on sale. That was my well-received contribution to the festivities.

I also went with Harold to the London Palladium, equivalent to our Palace Theater, for an evening's English Vaudeville presentation, which was far less sophisticated than similar entertainment in New York. Still, I enjoyed every minute of it. We had tea a couple of times in the famous Lyons Corner House(s) and I got pretty much into the swing of London life, insofar as I was only there for little more than a week and there was a war on.

The circle in which I traveled, thanks to Harold and Mabel, was very similar to our own group in East Midtown, which I had left in mid-1942. It was a great week and, as with all good things, it too quickly came to an end. On the last day I packed my things, having said my good-byes, and found my way back to Kings Cross and retraced my steps back to Castle Dawson, having on the Irish Sea an even rougher crossing back to Belfast (again I used the horizon trick). Coincidentally, in January of 1944, the Germans renewed their bombing of London, the so-called Baby Blitz. Fortunately, I missed that.

Little did I know at the time but my train trip was on December 29th, the day I became a father.

12

PREPARATIONS IN ENGLAND

Back in Ireland and feeling very good about the trip to London, I described it in great detail in letters to Alice. Most of the letters I had written since coming overseas were short on detail, mainly because of censorship, but in this case I was able to let it all hang out.

And shortly after returning, I was informed by a cable, which was routed by way of North Africa, that I had become a father of a healthy baby boy—"mother and child doing fine." After another brief period, I received a very long letter, laboriously and lovingly composed, detailing the hours leading up to the birth, the birth itself, and the immediate days afterward. The letter was (and is) a masterpiece. I received congratulations all around from the guys but there was little I could do by way of celebration. So, I was a papa!

The mail from now on assumed another dimension. We had the baby to write about. We had exchanged a lot of correspondence about what to name the child. We had agreed that, if it was a girl, it would be named Ruth after my mother who had died in 1932. (The other three grandparents were still alive). We wrote back and forth across the sea and finally settled on Joseph as the given name and for his middle name we had no difficulty agreeing on Lincoln, the man who we both felt was the greatest American in history. So Joseph Lincoln it was.

We weren't in Ireland too long before it became known that it was only a temporary base and that we would soon be going on to England. I assume we would have gone there directly from the Mediterranean but there was no base ready for us. Meanwhile training continued and the balance of the men took their furloughs. One happy occurrence during this period was the stopping off in Belfast of a touring company of "This Is The Army," written by Irving Berlin for this war and including Berlin himself singing "Oh, How I Hate To Get Up In The Morning," which he wrote for a similar show in 1918 during World War I. I and some of the other guys were able to scrounge tickets and we traveled to Belfast for the show, which I found to be very enjoyable.

Too much cannot be said about the various entertainers who made these USO-sponsored trips throughout the world to the various fighting fronts. Shows were put on not only in theaters as in Belfast, but many times on makeshift stages in remote locales. One such visit I recall was by Bob Hope, who may have done more of this than anyone else, who showed up on the fringes of the desert in North Africa together with a singer, Frances Langford. In this case he was scared half out of his wits as the 504th's committee that handled the arrangements planted some strategically located explosives, which were set off during various spots in the show. I must say, Hope took it well and a glorious time was had by all.

Then, toward the end of January, the word was that we indeed were going to England. And there was a party of one officer and two men from the Division who were going as an advance group to iron out the details of billeting, etc. My good friend Colonel Rusk was given the assignment as the officer in charge and I was one of the two men selected to go! How and why I was chosen I have no idea to this day. First, this was a personnel move and should rightly have been handled by G-1 or the Adjutant General, but it was given to the G-2 with enlisted personnel from G-3. The other man was Jack Rohr, a Pfc. Well, rightly or wrongly, we were off!

We flew to the English Midlands and were met and driven to Braunstone Park in the west end of Leicester, which became our home for the coming months. Braunstone Park was set down in the midst of a neighborhood of one-family homes reminiscent in many ways of blocks back in Queens. It was newer and built better than the older, downtown areas of the city. Leicester was a city of probably 200,000 people and its populace was busy working long shifts manufacturing munitions for the war.

There was a battalion of black soldiers occupying the huts in the park and they were the crew who were finishing up their job of preparing camps in Leicester and several other towns and cities, including Nottingham, for the 82d Airborne. When they left Braunstone Park, it became the home of Division Headquarters, our Military Police, the Medical Company and the Signal Company.

I accompanied Colonel Rusk when he made his call on the black commanding officer of the construction battalion, finding out that his name was Major Durwood! Now when Durwood Rusk, Louisiana born and bred, found that out he slipped into his best southern drawl, which he rarely used, and proceeded to interrogate the squirming major about his family background because, according to Rusk, there had to be some connection going back to the days of slavery. It was a mortifying experience to listen to this, but it was typically Rusk.

As it turned out, there was little or no work for Rohr or myself and I spent most of my time with a group of Army Engineers who had the seemingly fun task of traveling around England giving demonstrations and lectures on booby traps, demolitions and the like. Jack Rohr and I ate and slept with them in one end of a hut and became spectators to the endless pranks they played on one another with blasting caps, trigger devices, and all the other tools of their profession. But soon they left, as did the construction battalion, which went on to another assignment of preparing billets and camps as the American presence in England continued to swell.

Then the 82d moved to England and was finally settled around Leicester and Nottingham at the beginning of February 1944. Organizational changes were made, since the 504th Parachute Infantry and the rest of its combat team had been left in Italy (not to join us until just before we left for France). An Independent Brigade, consisting of the 507th and 508th Parachute Infantry Regiments and their auxiliary troops, became attached to the Division during this period, thus swelling the normal three infantry regiments to four.

Being stationed in the Midlands had a lot to do with subsequent events since the 101st Airborne was stationed in the south of England, near where most of the American forces were, while we were some hundreds of miles away. Plans for the upcoming invasion dictated that the glider elements of the 82d would have to be moved much closer to

France prior to D-day because of the range limitations of the towing aircraft. This turned out, on a personal level, to be all-important as this positioning possibly saved my life.

The positioning of the various forces in England indeed dictated much of the way the war played out. The British forces were on the left as you would face the Continent and we were on the right. This meant that the ultimate landings would, with each nation's forces being assigned the shortest route to France, have the British (and Canadians) on our left during the landings. Thus the British faced the enemy at Caen while the ultimate break-out in August would be on the American-held right to the south and west. The British strategy after the break-out was to strike through the northern (shortest) route to Germany, and this became a bitter strategic debate for the remainder of the war. The American position was to attack on all fronts rather than a concentration on one. More on this later.

We settled into the Midlands area and training began in earnest. Day and night exercises were scheduled, and under the driving supervision of Ridgway and Gavin (promoted to Brigadier General and Asst. Division Commander) the 82d was molded into one of the finest fighting organizations on earth. There was a shortage of aircraft and limitations as to what could be done at night in the air over a populated and frequently bombed country, but we did as much as could be squeezed out of the limited resources allotted to us.

A War Room was set up in two huts at Braunstone and they became the center for all planning related specifically to the upcoming invasion. Normal activities, such as troop training and exercises, were conducted from two other huts which were assigned to the G-3 section. At this time the enlisted section consisted of Dorant, Richard, myself, Pritikin, Morse, Lange, Rohr, Gilbertson and Jungclas. Morse wrote his way into trouble when he complained in a letter home of the differences between the officers' accommodations as compared to the men's. Since all mail was censored, the wrong officer read this letter and word of Morse's "heresy" reached someone who decided that he was not meant for the elevated environs of Division HQ. He was unceremoniously transferred out.

How I pitied my good buddy, Spotswood, who had to suffer the mood swings and nitpicking of our erstwhile G-3, Colonel Rusk.

September 1942. One week before entering the Army, Len and Alice
at Colebrook, Connecticut.

The Mediterranean at Bizerte, August 1943. L. to R.: Richard, Morse, Lebenson, Jungclas.

Bizerte, North Africa, August 1943. Kneeling, L. to R.: Richard, Jungclas. Standing, L. to R.: Mehrholz, Lange, Morse, Lebenson, Pritikin.

August 1943, Bizerte, North Africa. The author "at work."

To the Commander in chief of the allied Anglo American Forces.
(G.4960).
Siculiana which has given to america a large contingent of her sons, about three thousand; a good number of whom, american citizens, are at this moment residing here, Welcomes you, assuring you, that no military resistence will be found in its territory.
Gladly puts itself at your Orders.
Siculiana; July 17th 1943
For the People.
Rev. Salvatore Marino
an American Citizen

Distributed to the 82d Airborne Division in Sicily, July 1943. Author's collection.

Distributed to Allied forces on entry to Naples, September 1943. Author's collection.

Brothers,

after thirtynine months of war, pains and grieves; after twenty years of tiranny and inhumanity, after have been the innocent victims of the most perverce gang at the Government; to day, September 8 - 1943, we can cry at full voice our joy, our enthusiasm for your coming.

We can't express with words our pleasure, but only we kneel ourself to the ground to thank Good, who have permit us to see this day.

With you we have divided the sorrow of the war, with you we wish to divide the day of the big victory.

We wish to march with you, until the last day, against the enemy N. 1,

We will be worth of your expectation, we will be your allied of twentyfive years ago.

Hurra the allied
Hurra the free Italy

The commitee of antifascist
ex
fighters of the big war

Notes made by author after Giant briefing on September 3, 1943.
The plan was for the 82d "to land by air in airfields in and around
Rome to 'assist in the defense of Rome' against the Germans."
Fortunately, at the last minute from inside Rome, General Maxwell
Taylor was able to cancel the mission, which might well have been the
biggest airborne disaster of the war.
Author's collection.

April 1944. The author alongside glider prior to only training flight.

Braunstone Park, Leicester, March 1944. G-3 enlisted men, L. to R.: Unknown, Jungclas, Richard, Pritikin, Dorant, Wilhelm, Lebenson.

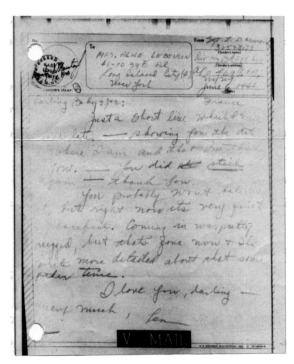

V-Mail hastily written by author to wife, Alice, on D-Day, June 6, 1944.
In it he says, "Right now it's very quiet. . . . Coming in was rugged but
that's gone now." If Alice could have seen the wreckage of her husband's
glider (below) she would have had cause for more alarm.

The author at the wreck of a D-Day glider outside Ste. Mere Eglise, June 1944.

The author seated on the landing gear of a Horsa glider, wrecked on D-Day in Normandy.

G-3 in Normandy, June 1944 during a lull. L. to R.: Wilhelm, Leonard, Lange, Dorant, Lebenson, MacPheeters, Adams, Marston, Graham.

The author outside Ste. Mere Eglise ca. D+3, June 1944. This was the town in which a paratrooper, still in harness, hung from a church steeple during the battle.

On a visit to Normandy in May 2005. The author at railroad track, the scene of D+1 adventure.

The author in 2005 at the grave of Pvt. Raymond Jungclas in the U.S. cemetery at Colleville-sur-Mere above Omaha Beach. The stone marks the date of death as June 15, 1944.

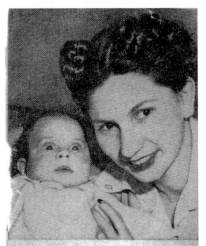

Joseph was born Dec. 29, 1943, to Mrs. Alice Lebenson of 4110 39th Place, Long Island City, Queens. His father, Tech. 4/g Leonard Lebenson, a draftsman, is with the airborne infantry in England.

Notice appeared in *PM* (New York newspaper), early 1944.

August 1944. After return from Normandy, meeting with brother Milton (left) in Manchester, England.

Remnants of elaborate covered hole dug by author in Dekkerwald near Nijmegen, Holland in Fall of 1944. Logs can still be seen over the trench in 1984.

Jan. 1945. Regroup time in the Ardennes. DeTomasso, Lange, Lebenson.

March 1945. Toohey and Lebenson at training jump near Reims, France.

Early 1945. General Gavin addressing group at parachute wings ceremony. In group are Spotswood, Lebenson and Lange.

May 1945. Meet the Russians! Ludwigslust, Germany. "Snips," Russian interpreter, is third from left; Lebenson is third from right.

May 1945. Grabow, Germany. The author on left, with group of Russian soldiers just after Germany's surrender.

The author, kneeling at left foreground, with a group of English, Russian and American soldiers. Ludwigslust, Germany.

May 1945. G-3 in victory, Ludwigslust, Germany.
Front row: Novak, Lekson, Lee, Norton, Ketterson, Smith. Second row: Hidalgo, Lebenson, DeTomasso, Fritz, Rohr. Third row: Bulleit, Sonday, Law, Lange, Gilbertson. Fourth row: Pritikin, Meyer, Wilhelm, Edison. Missing: Marston, Graham, Swope, Star.

May 1945. Ludwigslust, Germany.
General Gavin pinning Oak Leaf Cluster to Bronze Star on Len Lebenson.

With our gracious friends and hosts during our 2005 visit to Normandy.
Alice and Len with Henri-Jean and Yvette Renaud. Henri's father was the
wartime mayor of Ste. Mere Eglise, and he was a small boy when the 82d
paratroopers descended out of the night around his town on D-Day.

Len Lebenson and his wife, Alice, on his 80th birthday.

Family group in Quineville, Normandy in May 2005. From left:
Alice, daughter Ruth, grandson David, Len, son Marty, son Joe.

Planning for Normandy include countless studies, the fleshing out of intelligence capability, which in uded photo interpretation, language interpretation, prisoner interro ation, military government, intelligence gathering and counter-int igence activity. All this made the G-2 Section bulge at the seams and Rusk kept all these subgroups hopping with countless assignments.

Information was disseminated about enemy aircraft, armor, ordnance, secret weapons development, and various forms of uniforms and the ranks that went with them. One of the two War Rooms was devoted to this activity. Each morning Rusk had a parade of officers waiting their turn outside his cubicle to give their daily reports and receive their customary dressing-downs. It was comical and nauseating at the same time. All of the reports and paperwork and assignments of men to the various projects went through Jim Spotswood. What an assignment!

Compared to G-2, we at G-3 were in heaven. The new G-3, Bob Weinecke, was a composed, urbane executive from the business world and took the transfer from G-4 very much in stride. He came to us when Colonel Turner had a recurrence of his stomach bleeding and was sent back to the States. Sanity and a sense of humor, both of which Weinecke had to a great degree, prevailed, and we fortunately had none of the gut-wrenching nonsense that prevailed just next door. During this time, Lieutenant Graham joined us. Gerard and Marston were also with us throughout the planning period of early 1944.

The fact that all mail was censored was a source of annoyance to us but we kind of accepted the impersonal nature of the process (what else could we do?). But knowing that your letters were to be censored had the effect of inhibiting what one might otherwise write. As the war rolled on, two of our officers, Graham and Marston, stopped bothering to read our mail and just affixed their signatures to the envelopes as required, much to our delight.

Just before leaving for Normandy, the group was rejoined by Harold Wilhelm, who had been busted during the late days at Ft. Bragg, and whom we welcomed wholeheartedly. His rank was Private. We also were joined by Master Sergeant Leonard, who was the Operations Sgt. of the Independent Brigade, which had been folded into the 82d.

Along about mid-March, planning for Operation Overlord, the invasion of France, began in earnest. Dorant, Richard, Lange and I were given a very serious lecture about security and then were issued cards marked "Bigot," which gave us access to the War Rooms that were under 24-hour armed guard. The word "bigoted" was used throughout both ours and the British Armies to describe someone who had access to a high level of planning. The planning was indeed on a need-to-know basis, with us at the 82d having no need to know the details of, for example, the beaches assigned to the Canadians. Neither did we have knowledge of the use of Airborne troops in the British sector. We knew what we and the units on our immediate flanks were to do. We mainly knew that the invasion was going to be huge, and that we would play an important part.

So we did work in two different atmospheres: one being the normal training activities, which were conducted from the G-3 huts; the other being the Overlord planning in the War Room. Our instructions were to discuss planning activities only within the War Room. For example, if Richard and I were outside the War Room we could not discuss any of our work, even if we were completely alone. I believe that we carried out these instructions without exception—it became second nature as time went on. In later years, as I thought of the vast security problem and the great number of men who were privy to some detail of the plan, it is a source of amazement that there weren't any breaches of security. We were not confined to our base, and most of us spent time in town and in bars and mixed with the civilian population. And the situation that prevailed within the 82d probably was duplicated throughout the many organizations of the Army, Air Force and Navy. And yet, there were no breaches of security except for one officer who reportedly sent a copy of a plan to his father for safe-keeping!

The handful of enlisted men from G-2 and G-3 who were bigoted took turns at being Charge of Quarters at night in the War Room, which was manned around the clock, including weekends. Complementing the CQ was the OD, Officer of the Day, who was rotated for the duty, as we were. That duty, which came roughly once a week, was a reading bonanza because the various Intelligence Bulletins from SHAEF, US First Army, Army Air Force—mainly week-

ly publications, were on hand to be read. These detailed the results of
our bombing, including reports from the French Underground and
updates on the progress of the German Atlantic Wall fortifications,
snippets picked up about new enemy weapons development, and other
recent news. It was fascinating reading.

Our mission within the overall plan changed from time to time.
Each time there was a change, however slight, we had to adjust our
maps accordingly, and re-do in most cases the order of our planeloads
(each called a serial). We were constantly doing these revisions as
things became more refined as the date approached. In the last two
weeks our plan changed almost completely. Originally we had been
assigned to drop around St. Saveur le Vicomte, which is on the western side of the Cherbourg Peninsula. German troop movements into
the area, duly reported both by Air Force reconnaissance and the
French Underground, caused the plan to be changed and we to be concentrated around Ste. Mere Eglise, some few miles inland from Utah
Beach. We spent a feverish week on a new plan, working out all the
details, and publishing all the data and instructions.

An illuminating thing happened one Sunday while I was on duty
in the War Room. General Omar Bradley, the First Army commander,
was escorted into the premises by General Ridgway. They sat on a
bench facing a composite aerial photograph of the area into which we
were to be dropped into the battle, studying the photo and talking
about the upcoming fray. I couldn't help eavesdropping since we were
all in this relatively small room and it was impossible not to hear what
they were saying. They were doing a version of "what if," going over
the terrain and discussing the many possibilities, including both ours
and the enemy's situation. I found their knowledge of the problem
astounding and I witnessed what being a professional soldier with the
background of West Point meant. It was very impressive and I felt
good about our leadership.

At the same time, we also had our duties in the "normal" G-3
training routine, and we divided our time between the two aspects of
our lives—the planning and the training. We also had the opportunity
to go off the base in the evenings as work permitted. Trucks left the
camp after evening chow and dumped off the riders at the clock tower
in the center of Leicester. From there, choice of direction could lead

one to a pub or one of the two movie houses in the area. I had previously gone into town with those booby trap engineers, and we'd gone to a pub close to the clock tower, where I came to know some of the "locals." I continued to go there, perhaps once a week, for the duration of our stay in Leicester. Beer was strictly rationed to the pubs and they were only open for two hours in the afternoon and from 7 to 10 in the evening. Many times the beer ran out before 10 o'clock. Other times the barkeep's phrase "Time, gentlemen, time," signified the approach of 10 PM and the end of the flow of beer. The times were strictly kept. Then the procedure was reversed, and trucks deposited us back in camp. Remember, all of this was done in blackout conditions, which lent a mysterious air, particularly during the winter evenings when the smoke from all those open coal fires lay in the atmosphere.

There was a lot of beer drinking but very little drunkenness, perhaps because the pubs were limited in their fare. The men would straggle back to the barracks after a few hours of imbibing and fall into the sack. One of our men, Acolina, who was with the Finance Office, would invariably come back late from his forays and stagger over to the pot-bellied coal stove in the middle of our hut and promptly urinate into the box of ashes next to the stove. He always furiously denied this in the face of many adverse witnesses. Oddly enough, no revenge was ever extracted because Aco, when sober, was one of the best-liked guys in the barracks.

In 1969, when Alice and I took our first overseas vacation, we scheduled a stop in Leicester and stayed at the George Hotel, which was around the corner from the clock tower. One of the things I wanted to show was the pub I had spent many hours in but, to my dismay, it was no longer there, being replaced by some other store. What a disappointment!

Training was not without the usual incidents stemming from the exuberance and just plain strutting on the part of our troops, who were known for an intolerant attitude toward everybody else. This chip on the shoulder stance led to confrontations with other troops in and around the bars, resulting in some fracases in which there were serious injuries. So much so that the area command, an administrative branch, finally ordered that the entire division be confined to base.

Well, Ridgway would have none of that and, while sternly admonishing us against fighting, did not apply any restrictions against the men. Word in the army has a way of getting around, and by some kind of selection, other soldiers stopped frequenting Leicester, especially the bars and neighborhoods our men were known to use. So by this process an uneasy calm settled in and, after many weeks, all had been forgotten.

During the early days of the strained conditions, Pritikin came to me and asked me for the loan of my Beretta pistol, because he wanted to arm himself on a trip to town! I had purchased this for about $25 somewhere along the line and was not supposed to have it. I kept it in the bottom of my B bag (the barracks bag containing my little-used effects). I didn't know what Marv was planning but refrained from giving it to him. Apparently, others were arming themselves with firearms and trench knives for protection, all of which added to the volatility of those days.

One evening during this time while I was on duty in the G-3 hut, word came that the company officers (different from the staff officers with whom we worked), because of the arms-carrying incidents, were conducting a showdown inspection in the barracks. Now, the head-quarters and headquarters company men were billeted in a series of huts, each accommodating about 40 men, and the inspecting group was going through them one by one. In a showdown inspection, each man stood by his cot and emptied the entire contents of his A and B bags onto his cot for the inspecting crew.

I was in a dilemma because of the offending Beretta. I knew that my effects should not be inspected unless I was there, but one could not be completely sure of that. I made a decision, based on the numerical probability that they would be in a different hut from mine, and hurried back to the barracks, intending to remove the pistol and safely stow it somewhere in one of the G-3 huts. I burst in through the blackout doors at one end of the hut and to my horror saw that all the men were lined up alongside their beds with their stuff arranged on them! The inspecting crew, led by Captain Faith (now the Head-quarters commandant), were just beginning their job. I, with pounding heart, moved to my bunk which was in the center of the hut and, on an impulse, quickly wrestled the Beretta from the bottom of my bag, shoved it under my jacket and, just as quickly strode out of the rear doors of the hut and hurried to the safety of the G-3 hut. I had spoken to no one and no one spoke to me.

The next morning, at the conclusion of Reveille, Captain Faith called out, "Sergeant Lebenson, report to the Orderly Room." My doom was apparent! I went in as directed and there was Faith putting on that stone visage which is required for such occasions. He demanded that I explain my actions, leaving the barracks while the showdown was being conducted and avoiding being part of it. I summoned as innocent a look as possible, explained that I was on duty at G-3 at the time, and had only come back to the barracks to get some cigarettes and that "no one had told me that I was to be part of the inspection."

I was leaning on the well-known doctrine of not having to do something unless directly ordered and that one could be excused if ignorant of what was going on. Faith knew I was lying through my teeth but could do nothing about it unless he could prove I knew exactly what was going on. It was a close call. Later that morning, I explained the whole thing to Captain Marston, threw myself on his sympathies (which I just knew he would extend) and gave him the Beretta for safekeeping.

While in Leicester I met some friends of Harold and Mabel Goldman, namely Joe and Helen Pritchard, a local couple. He was an engineer who traveled about supervising the use of products manufactured by his firm. I spent many evenings with them. They were on the other side of town and I used a folding bicycle we had glommed onto at G-3, and pedaled my way to their home.

Mabel Goldman, who I had met in London, became pregnant and moved out of London and into her in-laws' home in Edgbaston, Birmingham. I visited her there one weekend, to the dismay of Harold's parents, who were not comfortable with a Yank in the house. Birmingham was interesting because at that time in 1944 it had been free of bombing for some time and seemed to be leading a normal existence. Getting back and forth from Leicester was simple because of the efficiency of the rail system.

As training intensified we had a couple of Command Post Exercises, called CPX. A written scenario would be produced, bringing into play the various functions of the CP—message receipt and delivery, a running journal, a battlefield map, issuance of orders and reports, the use of runners and liaison officers, "digging in," etc. The various headquarters would perform the functions as outlined in the scenario. The Signal Company would install telephone wires, which would be strung to the lower headquarters (regiment and battalion) and a close simulation to battle conditions would hopefully be achieved.

We had one large-scale glider exercise and I finally got to ride in a glider. I don't have too much recollection of the flight but I have a series of photographs, including one in which I am standing calm and entrepreneur-like alongside a glider. That exercise included most of the elements of the Division and, as the day for the great event grew closer, our degree of preparation increased.

Our OCS applications, meantime, were Dead on Arrival. Colonel Barrett finally convened his board so I went before it and was passed with flying colors—the only problem being that because of our state of readiness, all the applications had been frozen. It seemed it just wasn't to be. I would go through the war as an enlisted man. Richard fared better, being the recipient of some intervention from Washington—someone in his family had pulled some strings—and he left us to go back to the States for Judge Advocate School.

At the same time, Pritikin came down with some glandular problems and was in the hospital, so we were becoming, during this crucial period, somewhat short-handed. Fortunately, Wilhelm had rejoined us. So at the time of Normandy we had Dorant, myself, Wilhelm, Lange, Rohr, Jungclas, Gilbertson and Leonard (from the Airborne Brigade). Of the group, Rohr, Jungclas and I were draftsmen and Lange, Wilhelm, Gilbertson and I could type. Dorant had neither skill and Leonard soon left us in Normandy when there was a shortage in one of the Regiments.

Somewhere along the line it was decided that I would go in on D-Day as the one enlisted man from the section. The others would follow on the succeeding days. This was the decision of Colonel Weinecke, with whom I had achieved a very good working relationship. He, unlike the other staff officers, was not from West Point or a military college, but was in the insurance business in Chicago and had received his commission through his college ROTC program. He had

achieved a grasp of what it meant to be a staff officer. It was a pleasure to work with him and he was responsible for my subsequent
advancement.

All was in readiness.

13

READY TO GO!

On the eve of the invasion, a pause for some stock taking:

The organization I was fortuitously attached to was among the best in the Army. Many said the very best. This had to do with the caliber of our leaders, the volunteer nature of most of the formations, and our training and experience.

The 82d was led by two great General officers. Matthew B. Ridgway had been one of General Marshall's protégés in the War Plans Division (the most illustrious of this group being Eisenhower). Ridgway was a solidly built, hawk-visaged, no-nonsense soldier who turned out to be absolutely fearless, and who demanded the very best from his subordinates and their commands. He could scare the hell out of someone with a glance. He was also known for his prodigious memory—he never forgot a name or face. Later in his career, he was given command of the Eighth Army in Korea, and then replaced MacArthur after that commander had been fired by President Truman. Ridgway was also appointed Chief of Staff of the Army when Eisenhower was president.

Complementing Ridgway was the Assistant Division Commander, James Gavin, nicknamed Slim Jim by all. Later, according to Stephen Ambrose in "Citizen Soldiers," Gavin became "the most beloved Division commander in the ETO." Gavin's path through West Point started as a Private and he rose upward through the ranks. In appearance he approached the ideal of an All-American lad turned soldier. A slender six-footer, he had good looks and a feline grace. From the first days of action in Sicily it was apparent that he saw his place among

the front-line soldiers. He made a point of being with the lead battalions in every engagement and he became a familiar sight at the front
as he strode the battlefield carrying an M-1 rifle at his side. He was
adored by the men as he rose to take over after Ridgway's promotion
to Corps. After the war, Gavin became G-3 of the Army and Ambas-
sador to France.

Between the two—Ridgway and Gavin—our leadership going into
Normandy was second to none.

The individual paratrooper volunteered for many reasons.
Principally, the attraction was the chance to serve in an elite outfit
where physical fitness was the name of the game and where there was
a promise of high adventure in service to one's country. Some may
have joined for the extra fifty dollars a month, which doubled a
Private's pay. Then there were those who were in dead-end situations
and one of the only ways out was to volunteer for parachute school.
And finally there were the malcontents who came to us but were really never happy anywhere. Among this mix there were those who
scrapped within and without the unit, their bloodied heads considered
by some to be a badge of honor. A good bit of this was encouraged by
the officers. The Army's chore with this multi-faceted group was to
take it and mold it into fighting trim, doing so by assigning a cadre of
young, enthusiastic officers (also volunteers), and capping it off with
an energetic, professional leadership at battalion, regiment and division level. This they did very well.

The training was intensive, with concentration on physical fitness
through running, exhausting calisthenics, hand-to-hand combat drills
with exotic weapons, and the use of push-ups as a punishment tool.
The training schedule started early in the day and finished late. Units
competed with each other to prove which was in the best shape. A
professional knowledge and attitude toward the tools of the trade—
rifle, mortar, machine gun, bazooka, explosives, etc. had been instilled
in all ranks. The American paratrooper was resourceful and cunning,
trained to operate either as an individual or part of a group. What
stood out was the pride in self and unit—we darn well looked like soldiers, trim, eager and athletic, wearing our uniform as a badge.

In short, everybody felt fit and confident in the outfit's ability.
Now, how did all this show up in our headquarters, where we knew

that we would probably never be in a protracted firefight, where our weapons were typewriter, map, grease pencil, and telephone? Obviously we were not in the physical condition of the bulk of the men, but particularly after having gone through Sicily, Italy and the months up to Normandy, we were skilled and ready to go, also confident in our abilities. We dubbed ourselves "chairborne," only half in jest.

By this time I finally considered myself fit and ready to play my part in this great machine. I knew my job and had the respect of my fellows and superiors. I had gained the unofficial title of "operator," which meant I knew the rules and how to bend them. I had become a talented scrounger and hoarder of supplies, practicing thievery when necessary. This ability helped me carry out my job and also to avoid a great deal of the chicken shit that came with being a soldier. I had carried three stripes since January of 1943, and here it was May of 1944. My hopes of getting to OCS had been dashed by circumstances not of my doing. But when I was selected to be the one G-3 Sergeant to go in on D-Day I was not surprised because it was the logical choice. Actually, it gave me pride and something of a lift.

One of my little side adventures was attendance at Exercise Dart, which was held in Torquay toward the end of May. This exercise brought the commanders of all the major units taking part in the invasion together for a question-and-answer, "what if" session, testing the preparedness of the respective commanders. It was led by Field Marshal Montgomery, who was in charge of all the Allied land forces in the initial invasion. Ridgway was accompanied by Weinecke and Eaton and they brought along Lange and me from G-3, also McRae who was Ridgway's secretary. We brought copies of our Field Order and maps of our area of the battlefield showing our proposed dispositions. Willis and I stood in the back of the hall "at the ready" and in awe of all the heavy brass, but mostly listened to the goings-on.

Montgomery was there but said only a few words at the end of the session. One remarkable thing about this event for us was the gathering of the enlisted personnel in a Torquay resort hotel the night before the meeting. We had flown down from Leicester. There were guys there from all the American assault divisions, ditto the British and Canadian, plus all the smaller units such as the amphibious engineers, special tank groups and demolition men. Naturally, we did not talk any details but we all knew that this was a large "bigoted" group and we kind of sized each other up with interest. Lange kept looking for that elusive guy from Dubuque (Iowa), his hometown, a search he carried on throughout the war without success. The exercise was a one-day affair and we flew home as soon as it was over.

An interesting thing had happened earlier as told to me by Randy Strother. He was about the nicest guy in the outfit—he came from West Virginia and was attached to G-2. He was also the least soldierly looking of us all, being on the tubby side with his uniform always ill-fitting and clumsily worn. But Randy was universally liked. He told me that one day when he was on duty in the War Room he heard Colonel Weinecke discussing the G-3 personnel with another officer and Weinecke said, "Lebenson is about the best man I have. He's Jewish." I was somewhat taken aback by the reference to ethnicity, but Randy assured me Weinecke meant it as a compliment.

I have been asked many times since the war whether I felt any anti-Semitism directed against me, and I have always answered in the negative. I'm sure there was anti-Semitism around but there were also things said about Poles, Italians, the Irish, and others. I think there is some bigot in almost everybody but I repeat that, while I made no secret about being Jewish, I was never conscious of being the recipient of discriminatory comments or actions. There were only a few Jews in our outfit. Pritikin and I were in G-3; Brown and Sigman were in G-1. Those two were men with show business backgrounds and were responsible for entertainment programs. Kaplan was the chief NCO in the Adjutant General's office. That was about it. Although I didn't hang out or carouse with the guys, it wasn't because I was Jewish or because I was ostracized, but rather that I was one of the few married men in the outfit and wasn't on the lookout for girls. I spent many an evening with Kaplan and Sigman in the G-3 hut playing pinochle; coincidentally they were both Jews and pinochle players.

To get back to the story. As noted earlier, the glider elements of the Division were separated from the larger parachute formations because the distance from the Midlands to the battlefield was out of the limited range of the tow planes. Therefore we were bundled into trucks at the end of May and driven to the south of England and settled in around airfields that were also being used by the 101st Airborne Division. The entire southern rim of England bristled with men, equipment and munitions. This was apparent to the villagers, who knew the invasion must be near as they noted the endless convoys headed south, and we were everywhere sped on our way with cheers, thumbs-up signs and the like. It was a thrilling, once-in-a-lifetime scene in which all understood its gravity and importance, never again to be repeated.

There were 52 gliders assigned to the 82d Division for the initial assault, and a like number to the 101st. They were apportioned out very selectively. Space was given to the Glider Field Artillery, whose snub-nosed 75mm guns would be desperately needed, and also to the 57mm anti-tank guns of the Anti-Aircraft/Anti-Tank Battalion. Space was also allotted to the Signal Company and the Medical Company, leaving some room for Division Headquarters. We were bringing in a few jeeps and trailers as well as a skeleton staff (including me). I was assigned to a glider that would be carrying a trailer filled with supplies and, mainly, maps. I had carefully loaded the trailer with enough supplies and equipment—map board, jelly reproduction roll, sheets of acetate, 22" x 34" paper for producing daily situation reports, typewriter, blank journal sheets, pencils, hectograph and regular carbon paper, thumb tacks, grease pencils (most important!)—enough to function with as soon as we were able to establish a Command Post. Everyone had spent time and effort into calculating these loadings because of the limited space available with all the competing needs.

Some idea of the built-in difficulties to be faced can be seen when it is understood that we were going in in the dark, we had never had a night exercise, and that, for example, it was assumed that my glider would make a decent landing and we would be able to jack-ass the trailer out of the glider. Then we would still have to find the jeep that would tow us, assuming it had had a safe landing and was nearby. All this in the dark, possibly with enemy fire to be faced!

We settled into a designated field located somewhere in the crowded departure area and prepared for last-minute drawing of equipment, plus getting body and soul together. Fortunately we were not there for an extended period of time. Here, for us in Headquarters, came our usual dilemma of dual accountability. We were members of the staff but were assigned administratively to Headquarters Company, which was the support entity for Headquarters. While in this camp we received directions from HQ Co. rather than HQ. For me, this became further complicated when Jim Spotswood and I were taken from this encampment and brought to 101st headquarters, where Colonels Eaton, Wienecke and Rusk were staying. Our generals were in the Midlands with the parachute elements of the Division. The staff officers were at the 101st to be in position to react to any new information or change of plans. Spotswood and I were there for the obvious reason of being on tap if needed. So we sacked out with the 101st for a couple of days, basking in the attention we received as "battle hardened" men. We were comfortable enough and I remembered going to a movie one evening, although I don't remember what it was. Nobody slept more than a few fitful winks.

The original plan was for the seaborne invasion to be on the 5th of June with us going in on the night of the 4th. As has been well documented, there was a heavy downpour that day and night and the invasion was postponed for a day, leading to all kinds of frantic rearrangements, particularly to those men who were out in the Channel in invasion craft. The 5th of June arrived, quite cloudy and threatening, but the decision was made to go. In mid-afternoon, Jim and I returned to our encampment. There I found that no one in charge (Headquarters Company) knew where I had been those couple of days. I can't explain this foul-up because there were some of our G-3 Officers around, and also Dorant, who could have told them. At any rate, when they couldn't find me, Jungclas was assigned in my place to accompany the map trailer and I was de-assigned. At that point one might think (myself included) that this was a break and I wouldn't have to face the terrors of the initial invasion, but I was determined to go as planned and frantically made that known. Somehow a compromise was made and I was re-assigned, not to the original glider, but to one that was carrying the Division Artillery Commander, Colonel March, and other men from artillery. So, as it turned out, I was to go in with a strange group and not as had been planned.

Now I had to catch up with the other men, drawing ammunition, grenades, first aid kit, rations, and filling my canteen with water. Decisions had to be made about what to stick in pockets and in the field pack. We had to carry a blanket and shelter half, three days

worth of rations, a cartridge belt full of ammunition, an extra ban-
dolier of ammo hung around the neck, packs of cigarettes stuffed into
every niche, a camera (I had decided this was a must, and I carried an
old Kodak Brownie). I also brought a bunch of plain and grease pencils and small 3 x 5 message books. I had an M-1 rifle, bayonet,
entrenching shovel, canteen and cup, and mess kit. I also had a gas
mask and a plastic envelope to cover me in case of gas attack (we
threw these things away early in the game). There were extra socks
and underwear. I had a parachutist's escape kit which included a silk
map of France, some coins, a small compass and a tiny saw blade
encased in rubber so it could be placed in the rectum if captured, to be
used to cut one's way out of captivity(!). I wore an Olive Drab wool
uniform and a field jacket that were impregnated against gas. I sewed
the small invasion American flag on the arm of the field jacket. I also
carried a supply of V-Mail forms and writing paper, as I was determined to write home every day if possible. A flashlight rounded out
the burden. Covering everything, when fully loaded, was a yellow,
inflatable "Mae West" life jacket, to be used in the event of ditching
into the English Channel (pleasant thought).

We spent the last nervous hours lolling about, most of us feeling
feverish and excited. There was little conversation, but a lot of awkward banter. I later heard that in some company areas there were
fights brought on by the tension. In the early evening we were called
to a formation. In England at the time we were on double Daylight
Savings Time and it didn't get dark until almost 11 PM. Our line-up
was about 50 officers and men. We were given copies of Eisenhower's
Order of the Day, which was then read to us aloud (by this time we
were a very solemn assemblage). And then the invitation was made for
a moment of private prayer. I still had enough of the rebel in me to
reject that on a personal level and, while it seemed that all the others
bowed their heads in private reverie, I stood as straight as I could with
my head unbowed and simply called on the spiritual presence of Alice
to help me through whatever was to come.

We then loaded onto trucks for a short ride to the tarmac of the
airfield where the gliders and tow-ropes were lined up. It was then that
we noticed the invasion stripes which had been painted on all aircraft
in the last day or so to aid in identification and to prevent enemy air-

craft from impersonating ours. That added to the solemnity and special character of the occasion. On the short stroll from the truck to the glider I was assigned to, I had to stop twice to nervously urinate. (I was not the only one.) On the glider that would transport me to France were also Colonel Smiley, who was the Operations Officer of the Division Artillery, and Sgt. McFadden of the 80th Anti-Aircraft/Anti-Tank Battalion. I knew them both, so I wasn't completely alone. Ours was one of the very few gliders that flew only with personnel and not equipment such as a cannon, jeep or trailer. We were a group of fourteen, led by Colonel Andy March.

We self-consciously shuffled to our places, checked the seat belts, stowed our belongings as neatly as possible under the seats, which were bucket depressions in aluminum benches located one on each side of the glider. Most everybody was a smoker and all of us made sure that we had cigarettes handy for the trip. The glider itself was a utilitarian contraption, the outer skin being canvas, covering a frame made out of metal tubing. The floor was wooden. There were small plastic windows, but what everybody mostly noticed while seated in a glider were the control wires, which were everywhere in view going in all directions. These wires, in a crash, were lethal. Up front, the pilot and co-pilot had flimsy seats, windows to look out of and controls for flying the glider after it was released from the tow plane.

The gliders were generally referred to as "flying cigar boxes," attesting to their clumsy and frail appearance. The glider was towed by a long, inch-thick, nylon rope. Attached to the framework were first aid kits in neat zippered twill bags. (I later latched onto one of those, the bag going with me for the rest of the war as a container for soap, razor, comb, etc.) To round out the glider there was a small functional set of wheels up front and a stick-like skid in the rear. The pilot's compartment could be detached at floor level from the rest of the glider and be opened upward, exposing a yawning space to permit the exit of any vehicle it might be carrying. There was a small door in one side for entry or departure of passengers.

We quietly settled in, puffing on our cigarettes. Nightfall had just about come and we were ready to go!

14

D-DAY

We sat there, each man immersed in his own thoughts and fears. It was a humbling moment. We were all aware of the magnitude of what we were doing, and at the same time unwilling to go much beyond the personal concerns of body and soul. I have not yet met the guy who was part of the operation who didn't admit to some degree of fear just before take-off. Since fear, and at times sheer terror, will be part of the next days' events, it is fair to record that fear affected us all. What is called courage may be, simply put, the ability to function in the presence of fear. Some relatively few did fail to overcome it; but those who have known fear firsthand invariably understand and do not condemn those who came up short

For me, the quiet in those moments before take-off was accentuated because I really didn't know the guys I was with (except McFadden), so I didn't have the ability to exchange nervous banter, sarcastic remarks and insults as I would have with men I knew.

Finally the engines coughed and sputtered, then caught with a roar and we were nearly ready! The lingering small hope that somehow the whole thing might be called off because the enemy saw the light and surrendered was a non-starter. All systems were go and the inexorable process took over. Slowly the tow plane started down the runway, the tow rope extended to its full length, and with a small lurch we were moving, picking up speed and finally airborne!

As tightened up as I was after two sleepless nights (including the night before the one-day postponement of D-Day), feeling nervous and jumpy, all that mixture of uncertainty and fear just disappeared when the plane left the ground. At that moment I honestly felt an emotion akin to calm mixed with elation that we were finally on the way. Hard to explain, but true.

The sky armada fell into place in the planned formation of V-shaped echelons and we headed out over the Channel, knowing that beneath us was a mighty phalanx of ships and men. The debacle in Sicily when part of the 504th was shot down approaching landfall over our fleet dictated that we would not fly in over the invasion beaches. So the flight pattern was to take us west to the north of Cherbourg, use the Channel Islands of Jersey and Guernsey as beacons, and then turn south parallel to the west coast of the Cherbourg (also called the Cotentin) Peninsula. When we reached a line perpendicular to the landing areas, we were to turn again to the left, now headed east, aiming for our respective landing zones, which had been meticulously selected for tactical reasons.

It was a clear night along the sixty miles of the invasion beaches with the British 6th Airborne division on the eastern end and we and the 101st on the west. We could make out the shadows of ships in the water when we first took off and clearly saw the wingtips of the planes in our formation as well as the stars in the cloudless sky. It was just as planned until the unthinkable happened as we crossed the French shoreline, and we found ourselves immersed in a dense cloudbank! It was totally unexpected, scary and we were in the only part of the beachhead area to be so afflicted.

Further complications as we dodged in and out of the clouds came from a concentrated barrage of anti-aircraft fire, the enemy having been alerted by the earlier flight group. This, of course, was a new experience for me, partly fascinating because of the graceful arcing of the red and yellow tracers that filled the sky along with occasional explosions. Our smooth flight had become bumpy as the pilots, having lost formation in the clouds, sought relief from the dangers of mid-air collision and the flak by dodging left and right and up and down. We had no idea how menacing the flak was because of its novelty but knew there was danger in it. Fortunately, the run over land was only to be a relatively few minutes before cutting loose and then, praise be, we were disconnected from the tow without having been hit and we were gliding free. The moment of cutting loose is accompanied by a sudden stop of the noise and vibrations inherent with being towed, and suddenly the only noise is the whisper of the air as the glider passes through it.

It would only be seconds before landing as I checked my equipment as best I could, remembering the location of the seat belt release, my pack and rifle, and the exit door. Visibility was zero, moonlight being blocked by the clouds. We hoped to land in an open field but nevertheless braced for an impact. We were descending rapidly and suddenly there was a sharp plunge upward as the pilot desperately pulled up to avoid something. This was followed by a pancaking down and then we tore with a splintering crash against some kind of building, were spun violently around, and came to rest with another impact against still another object. After the final crash there was a brief moment of quiet. We certainly had arrived with a bang!

Taking immediate stock, finding no broken bones, I joined the rest in a controlled rush and clatter to get out the door. We were in France! More to the point, we found ourselves, once we became oriented and accustomed to the darkness, in a small field near a house and shed and a row of hedges. That is all we could immediately see. The pilot had seen the house in time to avoid it (the upward motion) but had smashed through the shed and finally the glider had hit and come to rest against a tree. It was crumpled and broken but, miraculously, we all came out in one piece. A moment of panic! I had lost my helmet. I rushed back into the remains of the glider and retrieved it. Actually, I also had a black eye, which came from whatever knocked my helmet off. I hadn't been conscious of any blow.

It was eerily quiet. We could hear some small arms fire off in the near distance but nothing else. Our voices were low to each other as we sought our orientation. It was still dark and the naval bombardment that was to accompany the seaborne landings hadn't started. But then came a noise which caused us all to become immediately alert. It came from the other side of the row of hedges and we soon discovered it was from an 82d paratrooper who had dragged himself there on a fractured ankle, broken on landing. He had been there for some time, perhaps an hour, and advised us that we were near a road and that there had been sounds of a pitched battle that had ceased only moments before we landed.

It took us only a few minutes to gather our things, check our rifles and ammunition, and prepare to move. But we were not a tactical unit with an immediate fire mission. We had the Division Artillery Commander, his Operations Officer, some officers from the anti-tank battalion and a smattering of enlisted men like myself who had varying assignments. My directive was to find the Division Command Post which was supposed to be located west of Ste. Mere Eglise. Division Artillery was not to be located near the CP, so I knew at some point I would have to leave this group and go on my own. But Colonel March took over and decided, after consultation with Colonel Smiley, that we would march down the road in the direction of the small arms fire. We formed into a loose column, rifles at the ready, with a spacing of a few yards between each man. Off we went—I was the last man in the column, wondering what might be behind me!

I checked the ammunition clip in my rifle and the loaded round in the chamber and made sure the safety was off. I also checked the grenades I had hanging on the front straps of my pack harness to make sure I could get at them, just in case. We moved out slowly, extending the column as we did, picked up some speed and marched down the road as quietly as we could. The noise of battle increased as we moved along and after about 10 or 15 minutes we were amidst a built up area of small houses, each surrounded by a fence. We met some of our paratroopers and also some civilians who were quietly moving about outside their homes. I had this impression of dead serious, poorly dressed men in shapeless peaked caps moving in the shadows. Very European in appearance. There was a lot of whispering going on and conversation was in hushed tones. We soon found out to our relief that we were in Ste. Mere Eglise, which was more or less our objective. Our troopers had landed earlier and there had been a pitched battle for the town, which was now in our hands—as it turned out, the first town liberated in France.

It was still dark but the horizon was showing some streaks of light and I decided to detach myself and head toward where our CP was to be established. This meant, after orienting myself based on what meager information I could get, going back on the same road on which we'd come into town, working my way into the area of farm fields and there, hopefully, I would find our group. Actually, by some kind of miracle we had landed almost exactly where we were supposed to. As it turned out, we were one of the few gliders (or sticks of paratroopers) who did.

So off I went as day was breaking. Almost at the same time the Navy opened up its pre-assault bombardment, which was earthshaking even where we were, though it was aimed at the area just behind the invasion beaches some miles away.

Being on my own was a daunting experience as I slowly picked my way through the fields and hedges. I did not walk along the road, feeling there was safety in the cover of the hedges. The occasional field had cows, many of them dead and many of them mooing uncomfortably as their milking time had passed. I saw only a few of our men and we warily sized each other up until firm identification was made. Daylight meant it was OK to smoke and I lit one after another. I knew the proposed location of the CP, about a mile west of Ste. Mere Eglise, not far from the road on which I had already walked. About two to three hours after landing, which included my detour into the town, I stumbled upon the field where I happily saw a few familiar faces. It was the CP! We were located in a field probably about 100 yards by 200 yards, close by a compound, which included a farmhouse and outbuildings. The field was ringed on all four sides by hedges and ditches and there was a row of apple trees down one side.

I wearily disposed of my pack, sat down and opened up one of the K-rations, which I gobbled down. There initially wasn't too much to do. Ridgway had been there; Colonel Rusk and Major Zinn were there. Sgt. Ramsey from the Chief of Staff Office was there, as was Vines from G-2. No sign of Jungclas from my group (he who had taken my place with the glider carrying the map trailer). A number of Headquarters Company guys were there, but we had no vehicles, radio or telephone. Communications were verbal or through the written message forms delivered by hand. A few glider pilots showed up, each of them with a hair-raising story. From what we could initially gather, the drops and landings had been all over the lot and our men were scattered throughout the peninsula.

We gravitated to one side of the field, near the apple trees and started to dig in to provide cover in case of attack. By late morning enemy activity had grown. Artillery fire was ranging in on the area we held around Ste. Mere Eglise, and the sound of small arms fire increased. At the time there were two fierce battles going on, one to the north of Ste. Mere and one in the other direction around La Fiere. We had become more of a center of activity. Couriers came and went, Ridgway was in and out, as always firmly in command. Our contingent built up slowly but still I was the only one, officer or enlisted man, representing G-3. I had no materials, so could not establish an operations map nor record the messages coming in and out. I occupied myself by digging in and helping out where I could, relaying bits of information, collecting others and keeping myself in readiness.

As the day wore on, reports were coming in testifying to the dispersal of the dropped troopers, battles fought and rumors about the beach landings. One thing was visually obvious and completely comforting—we had control of the air. Our fighter planes patrolled overhead, swooping up and down gracefully and acrobatically. The Luftwaffe was nowhere to be seen. That was immensely comforting but did not solve the immediate problem at hand. The fire around us at times became deadly. The enemy must have had some clue about where we were because the artillery and mortar fire became more concentrated, causing a few casualties, including Sgt. Ramsey, who was wounded only a few yards from where I was crouching in the ditch. We found the ditches along the sides of the field to be the preferred cover against the ever-increasing shrapnel. The scene became hectic with crouching bodies, hurried communications during lulls, and deadly, terrifying fire which made me hug the ground while willing my body into as small a ball as possible, covering my head while knowing that parts of my body were particularly vulnerable. All this was followed by intense relief when the fire let up, if only momentarily.

While this intense bombardment was going on, an incredible scene developed. One of the G-2 people was Staff Sgt. Vines, who was a cousin of a famous tennis star of the day, Ellsworth Vines. He was about the same size and looked like the star but our Vines didn't like his claim to fame being his cousin and usually became annoyed at the constant references he had to listen to. But there we were, in this field under fire, hunkering in the hastily dug holes and ditches, handling the spotty message and other traffic going in and out. With Colonel Rusk as G-2 there would be a guaranteed large amount going out. The

Army had these small 3 x 5 message books in which messages could be inscribed, with the original messages being delivered by hand. The artillery was hounding us, messages were coming in and out and there was a build-up of discarded carbon paper and tissue slips on the ground, particularly in the area where Rusk and Vines were operating.

During a lull in the shelling, Rusk called out, "Vines! Police up the area!" Meaning, pick up all the scraps of paper. There was no response from Vines, who was half huddled in his hole. The order was repeated just as some shells came whistling in. Still no response from Vines. Now came the ultimate warning: "Vines, this is a direct order, police the area!" Finally came an expletive-laden answer in a quavering voice from Vines, essentially "Pick them up yourself." If one can imagine a hush coming over an area under fire, one came to our apple orchard. By disobeying a direct order, Vines had committed an offense subject to court martial and imprisonment. But Rusk, perhaps realizing that his testimony would be required in a hearing and that his ordering a man to pick up scraps of paper while under artillery fire would raise eyebrows, perhaps in the wrong places, swallowed hard (I assume) and elected not to press the case. But then, suddenly, in a day or two, Vines disappeared, transferred to some unknown locale— unlikely proof that the way to get somewhere is to tell your superior officer off. But Rusk had to suffer the ignominy of having been told off and not having done anything about it. One could be sure that everybody, up and down the ranks, heard of it.

By now small arms fire was coming closer. Major Zinn was shot in the eye and was a casualty for the rest of the war. Others as well. There was talk of forming a skirmish line in the event the battle came up to our field, but it never did. We became increasingly alert to the thump, whistle, then screech of the fire as it descended upon us—never became used to it, but were becoming a little more adept about time, direction amd landing area. Toward late afternoon there was a lull.

In the meantime, our headquarters had grown, particularly with G-2 men. The ridiculous scene between Colonel Rusk and Sgt. Vines happened during this day. General Gavin, who was deputized as the initial commander of the parachute force, had not appeared in the CP or, if he had, not at the same time as Ridgway, who was ranging around the battlefield with his usual intensity. The day wore on with us knowing that, yes, we had made the landings, but we were dispersed and fighting some fierce peripheral battles. We had also taken the town of Ste. Mere, and our air force obviously commanded the skies. Most important of all, beyond having heard the tremendous naval bombardment on the beaches, we did not know how successful the landings had been, since there had been no contact between us and the seaborne force.

The day had become a jumble of rumor, hopes and periods of intense fire raining down on us, surrounding some spaces of relative calm. Through it all, there was a feeling of confidence that we would prevail. The farmhouse close by had a well which was used for drinking water. It also served as an early first aid station for the growing numbers of our wounded being gathered there during the day. It also became a collecting point for prisoners, who didn't look much like supermen. The Command Post had become and served as a message center, a place for hurried meetings, and the collection of fact and rumor. The day drew to a close and, with it, a slight cessation of activity; the artillery bombardment slacked off.

Night finally fell on a tired but upbeat group of about 20 officers and men. We agreed that each of us would take an hour's watch while the rest of the group would hopefully get some sleep. There was a large piece of tarpaulin which had been the outer wrap of an equipment bundle parachuted down and, after my turn on watch, I lit a cigarette while crouched underneath the tarp so as not to show light. The next thing I knew it was morning and I was awake in its chill with the crackle of artillery fire in the air. I had fallen asleep with the lit cigarette in my mouth. Like many others, I had gone at least 72 hours without sleep up to the night of D-Day. It was a wonder how we could function—and it was even worse for the men in the invasion craft at sea; they'd had to contend with seasickness in addition to the same lack of sleep.

The first day was an adventure in protecting body and soul, of heightened sensibilities, and of fear while realizing the magnitude of what we were doing. I had been more or less an odd man out since I had no materials to work with and the headquarters existed only in outline form. I had kept busy but still had to get back to my normal functions. I was the only G-3 person in the area. No word of Colonel

Weinecke or of Jungclas and the trailer. This, of course, would change.

We felt a certain pride in that we had made it, and that the power of our nation was behind us. D-Day had come and gone and we (the 82d at least) was lodged firmly in France. The day had been long and had moments of danger, but also moments of satisfaction as we realized that our force was consolidating and would only get stronger. I had managed to quickly write a V-Mail message to Alice commemorating the event, and folded it up knowing that it would be some days before it would be able to be mailed.

There was to be a glider follow-up on D+1 that would include the bulk of the 325th Infantry, the balance of the Artillery, Engineers, Medics, Engineers and Signallers, as well as some of our G-3 contingent, including jeeps, trailers and supplies. My recollection is that this event took place late in the afternoon, but have also read it was in the morning. In any event, it happened and was an awesome sight, seeing the sky full of aircraft towing gliders and watching their release and slow, graceful descent.

Before this happened I was approached by one of Ridgway's aides who directed as follows: General Gavin was reported to be located in a building alongside a railroad some mile or so from where we were. The route to him was to take a road bordering a neighboring field (not the road to Ste. Mere Eglise), follow it north to a railroad where this road crossed it on a bridge, go down to the tracks and follow them east to a grade crossing, turn left and on the road there would be a couple of buildings. In one of these, General Gavin might be found. If so, I was to report to him and summon him to the CP in the name of General Ridgway.

Gulp! This, as we liked to say, was no drill. I was to make this little jaunt by myself, across terrain that might not be occupied by us, and if so, in plain sight of any German soldiers. I gave consideration to faking it, hiding out for a while, and then reporting that I had lost the way. But I was already on my way even as I was turning over this possibility. At the road leading to the railroad, there was a 57mm anti-tank gun with its crew aiming the gun down the center of the road. So at least one of our glider-borne guns had made it! I remember thinking that they were in a very exposed position. We exchanged a few words, they being somewhat incredulous that I was going down that road on my own. Well, I was armed with my loaded rifle, extra ammunition and a couple of grenades. Would that be enough?

I walked down the edge of the road, uncomfortably alone, all my senses on the alert, and reached the railroad, which ran in a cut below the surrounding terrain. I was surprised at how up to date it looked. There were two sets of rails fading out into the distance in both directions. The track borders were free of debris and there was rock ballast on each side of the rails. The road I was on crossed the tracks on a bridge. Well, there was nothing for it but to keep going and I made my way down onto the tracks and headed to the right as directed. Still no sight of friend or foe. For cover, I decided to walk through the woods parallel to the tracks, but after stumbling through them for a short while decided that I was no safer there and my progress would be so slow that it would be better to go back down and walk along the tracks. (A decision that, years later, seems to have been foolhardy). I walked along the tracks, perhaps for a half a mile, to the crossing I was told I would find, and there I made the directed left turn onto a road which led a short distance to a cluster of buildings. Around them, to my great relief, were some of our men. It had been a hairy experience.

Inside there was a gaggle of men including Colonel Weinecke, but not Gavin, who had been there but gone again. I reported to Weinecke and told him why I had come and he immediately got ready to accompany me back to the CP. He had been there since early in the day and had no idea of where the rest of us were located. He collected Colonel Lindstrom, the Division Surgeon, and off we went, retracing the steps I had taken earlier. On the way, on the railroad tracks, we met Gavin, who was hurrying along with his bodyguard in the opposite direction. After a brief confab among the brass, I led the way back to the Command Post, ending the mission for which I later received the Bronze Star.

At about now the glider reinforcements came and, after a time, the CP became swollen with arriving groups who looked as excited as we had some 36 hours earlier to be greeted by us "grizzled veterans." Captains Gerard and Marston showed up, as did Dorant, Wilhelm and Rohr. Most important, we now had a couple of jeeps, trailers and all-important supplies. I immediately got to work assembling a 1:

25,000 map of the immediate area around Ste. Mere Eglise and began spotting our locations, fragmentary as the reports still were at the time. We were in business.

Contact had been made during the day with some advanced patrols of the 4th Infantry Division which had come in over Utah Beach. That cheering news came as we were just starting to function. I set up a map and we started to record events as they happened. Either this day or the next we produced our first Situation Report. Orders were still being issued verbally to the beleaguered units, many of them by Generals Ridgway and Gavin personally, as both generals were demonstrating their fearless manner of leadership. About this time word came that Jungclas was either injured or wounded and was in a German Field Hospital. I never established how that news arrived; it had to be either by a glider pilot or someone from Headquarters Company who had been on Jungclas' glider. The trailer, or course, was lost. I treated the news as any other rumor—skeptically—but I could not avoid the thought that there, but for the grace of God . . .

We were still under almost constant artillery fire but were learning how to use cover, also to be constantly aware of where the cover was. We were close to the earth and living, eating, washing, sleeping, moving one's bowels, etc., under the ever-present awareness that we were on a battlefield. The well in the farmyard ran dry about this time so we had to husband the water we had until a more adequate supply was found. The farm was bursting with our wounded and also with prisoners, who included some very young kids and some Asians who we took to be Mongolians.

The initial phase for us at G-3 was over and the rest of the battle lay ahead.

15

NORMANDY

The second day of the invasion was drawing to a close. It was still an exhilarating feeling to actually be a part of the entry into Europe, after so much training, delay, anticipation and hope. After two days in France it seemed safe to say we had been successful in making a lodgment; whether we could maintain, solidify and then extend our foothold would depend on what the surprised Germans could throw against us.

The battlefield was taking shape. We were developing cohesion, even with our numbers reduced due to the erratic landings and in spite of the frantic efforts of the enemy to dislodge us. Where leaders fell or were absent, others stepped forward or were given the order to assume areas of responsibility. It was working. Though no longer at full strength, we were "whole."

For the next month, during which we were in constant contact with the enemy, the Division fought a series of engagements, some desperate in nature, always holding any ground that had been won and fulfilling our assignments. We spearheaded the move that cut the Peninsula in half and isolated the German-held area in the north from the rest of the battlefield. We turned south and advanced to a line from which we were relieved after the 4th of July, the line which became the starting point leading to the breakout in August from St. Lo. The fighting caliber of the Division and the heroic mettle of its officers and men showed itself to be unsurpassed by any other formation, even though we were seriously understrength. I felt proud and awed to be a part, however small, of this force. On those occasions when supported by attached Corps artillery and armor, we were unstoppable. When we were finally withdrawn in July to return to England for refitting, our numbers had dwindled in some cases to skeleton formations, and we were in dire need of rest and re-formation.

Too much cannot be said about Ridgway and Gavin for their leadership during this period. They both ranged the battle areas tirelessly, supporting and urging the forward formations in their efforts. Their attitude was infectious. They could also be demanding and firm in their expectations.

Once, in my hearing range, Ridgway called aside the liaison officer from the 507th during the early days of the invasion. The 507th was having a particularly difficult time, having been landed poorly, and it had suffered almost the complete loss of its regimental leadership. This woebegone, stubble-faced lieutenant was reporting verbally to all who would listen the dire situation of the 507th, telling how badly they were faring on all sides.

Taking the lieutenant away from the small gathering of men around our G-3 location, Ridgway said to him, "Lieutenant, if I ever hear you talk in this manner again, I will bust you so hard and so fast, you will bounce." The edge of his voice was so hard it gives me chills to this day, almost a lifetime later.

Another time, some weeks later, we were in the hills above La Haye du Puits in what was to be our last engagement in Normandy. Our directive from Corps was to clear an area which included the taking of some hills and woods. The 508th had essentially been ordered to reach a certain line after a night's fighting, at which time we would have completed our task in Normandy and be relieved. The 508th had also been decimated in the initial landings, and subsequent heavy engagements had brought them considerably below strength.

We had our forward Command Post in the kitchen of a farmhouse and I was working on the journal at one end of a long table. At the other end, General Ridgway was talking to Colonel Lundquist, commander of the 508th, via field telephone. The Colonel was registering his objections and reservations about the coming engagement, pleading the case for his undermanned regiment. Again, with the same steel in his voice, Ridgway said, "I'm sorry, Roy. The order stands. The attack goes. Tomorrow morning, the only Germans in those woods will be dead Germans." And that's exactly what happened.

But one should understand that Ridgway (and Gavin) did not give orders like that and then turn around and put their feet on the desk. They would be on hand at the jump-off and attack points and would stay throughout the engagements to offer their help, advice and leadership.

One earlier morning, I was alongside the ditch in which I slept, shaving. Shaving entailed a little planning and initiative. We had Coleman stoves, which were cylindrical—about 4 inches in diameter and 12 inches high. When the bottom tank was filled with gasoline, it could be pumped and if the gods smiled favorably, would be lit with a ring of flame about 3 inches in diameter. The main problem with those stoves was that they were meant for unleaded gas, which we didn't have, so getting them to work was touch and go. Once lit, a helmet full of water could be precariously balanced over the burner and heated. And voila, could be used for washing and shaving—also, on occasion for bathing the whole body using a sock as washcloth. Anyway, I was shaving, using my Rolls razor and tin mirror, and I must have looked pretty forlorn, because I saw out of the corner of my eye that Ridgway had materialized, and over he came with a D ration bar (concentrated chocolate), tossing it in my direction. "Good morning, sergeant," he said, and walked on, leaving me a little flabbergasted.

On another occasion, an emergency meeting of Regimental commanders was called to discuss details of an operation to be executed immediately, without the normal notice and preparation. As it happened, McRae, who was assigned to the Chief of Staff and was an excellent stenographer, was not to be found and Weinecke put in a rush call for me to come and take notes of the meeting. When the meeting was assembled, Ridgway began by citing the scope of the attack, the units to be used, and then stopped and said to me, "Are you getting this, Sergeant?" I said I was and he asked me to read it back. All I had were some scribbled notes, far from verbatim, but I gave it back as best I could. Weinecke gave me a wink, Ridgway nodded, and then proceeded. Luckily, the whole order was only several paragraphs. As soon as the meeting was disbanded I rushed over to my "office" and wrote the details out in longhand, trusting my memory. Then I got hold of a typewriter and made a workable copy, which I showed to Weinecke. He OK'd it and told me Ridgway knew I wasn't a steno but proceeded with me based on Weinecke's assurances that I would get it right. He told me Ridgway would remember.

Surprisingly, it wasn't too difficult to live on (and in) the earth. My pack, which could accommodate my blanket and shelter half, was always close at hand. In the pack I kept cigarettes, mess kit and some rations, the camera I had lugged to France, and a change of socks. I don't remember if I had spare underwear. I always had extra toilet paper (still from the rolls I had taken from the *Monrovia* on the shores of Sicily) and a length of rope from the same place.

In the location mentioned above where I was shaving, I had lined the bottom of one of the hedgerow ditches with soft branches, overlaid by my blanket. My pack was at one end and my shelter half was stretched over the ditch on a slant from the hedgerow for cover in case of rain. I also had a Mae West, the inflatable life vest, which was given to every soldier who came in by sea or by air over the beaches. This could be blown up by mouth and was used as a pillow. It was comfortable enough. Eating was done on the fly when time and inclination dictated.

C-rations were heated in the can the same way as the shaving water, over the Coleman stove. We usually had a couple of five-gallon cans of water around the area, which could be used for washing, coffee and cleaning up. Cleaning up and disposing of garbage would become a problem, particularly if we were in one place for more than a day or so. Moving one's bowels was a major concern. I never lost some sense of the need for privacy and there was always the fear, shared universally, of being caught under fire "with one's pants down."

I also found some time each day to write a few lines home. Sometimes it meant holding onto the letters for a few days before they could be mailed, but they all eventually were. I managed to put together some longer letters, trying to a give a sense of what it had been like. Like most men, I did not let the downside — the fear, dirt and danger, get into the letters home.

We established our CP at about six to eight different locations during the battle for Normandy. This meant we became quite adept at packing and moving. Our moves were always in two stages: an advance group first, followed by the remainder. Willis Lange and I were always the advance, to be followed in a matter of hours or days by Dorant, Wilhelm and Rohr. Now, Dorant was very aware of not being in the advance group and knew that he really should have been there—but since his skills were supervisory rather than "hands on," he was left behind.

Upon notification we were to move, we would pack a jeep trailer with map board, small field table, journal materials, maps, water, gasoline, rations, field packs, weapons, typewriter, paper, carbon and pencils, the smaller items being stowed in a couple of wooden ammunition boxes. We could do this, literally, in a few minutes. On arrival at the new location, we could also be back "in business" within a relatively short time. At some point the Signal Corps guys would come with a field telephone line, and sometimes with an electric line and bulb, which would be powered by a portable generator. Otherwise we worked with candles and flashlights. We also had Coleman lanterns, which usually were non-operative.

The forward CP would always be established in a farmhouse because we didn't have tenting capabilities with us. When the main body arrived we would have our blackout tent erected and we would operate out of a field close by a road. It was a decision by Ridgway that we didn't use towns for our headquarters, for two reasons. One, they were logical places to stay and therefore more liable to be sniffed out by the enemy, and two, towns were more liable to road jams because of cross traffic. Gavin also followed this procedure after he took over, the only exception being during the Battle of the Bulge, when weather conditions forced us indoors, though never in a town.

During this period, Willis Lange and I became very close and stayed that way for the duration. Willis came from Dubuque, Iowa, and was one of the few married men in the outfit. He was a rapid-fire typist and very easy to work with when we were under the challenge and rigors of a combat situation. Our cooperation with each other was based on mutual respect and knowledge of each other's capabilities. When there was a forward CP, Willis and I manned it. In one period we were in the same location for several days, operating out of the kitchen of a farmhouse. We dug a hole outside, lined it with blankets, and alternately slept in it while the other was on duty. When we broke the CP and removed our things from the hole we found we'd been sharing space with a slithering black snake! Willis and I campaigned together from Africa through Germany, through all the engagements. Efforts to get in touch with him after the war, undertaken too many years later, turned up empty, to my disappointment.

When we were reunited as a group, our routine centered around the map, the daily reports, the issuance and receipt of orders, and the keeping of the all-important journal. The time for each day's Situation Report was fixed at midnight. Each of the lower formations (Regiments, etc.) was required to get their reports to us by midnight so that they could be collated and brought into the Division's nightly report. The Situation report was always accompanied by an overlay of the Situation Map and would be reproduced by the hectograph (Ditto) method. The 22 x 34-inch master sheet would be put together and would consist of the map overlay (done with hectograph pencil) and pertinent typed material (which was done on paper with hectograph carbon paper). We then transferred this image to a moistened jelly sheet, which came as a 24-inch wide roll and would be unrolled to a receptive spot. The image would be absorbed onto the 1/4-inch thick hardened jelly and, in use, the image would be transferred to successive blank sheets of paper. After use, the unused hectograph image would sink into the jellied sheet so that the same spot could be reused in a few days. The usual run was about 50, which was more or less the distribution, at which time the master was pretty well faded.

This was all done either by a single electric light bulb in a blackout tent or by candlelight augmented by flashlight. Likely as not there would be artillery fire in the neighborhood and the need to keep absolute blackout conditions. The distribution of the reports was by courier or liaison officer.

Another duty, which I have referred to before, was the maintenance of our Operations Map. On a piece of plywood about 4-foot square, we would assemble a 1:25,000 scale map which covered our immediate battlefield. This map came in sections which we would thumbtack on the board, all of it to be covered by a sheet of clear acetate. Writing on this surface was by way of grease pencil, one of our most precious commodities. On the scale of the map, one half-inch would equal slightly less than 1,100 feet, and two and a half inches would roughly equal a mile. (In that scale the whole United States would cover an area the size of two football fields). The position of our Division would be represented more or less in the center of the map, with room to have the neighboring units shown on each of our flanks.

The map was divided into squares 1,000 meters on a side. There were numbered markings on each side of the map reading from left to right and from down to up. Each map had its own number, so that any location could be called out in writing by giving the specific country, scale, map number and horizontal and vertical coordinates (horizontal first). For example: "France, 1:25,000, sheet 2526, coordinates 150107." Assuming that the numbered markings on the sides of the sheet began with zero (0), this would locate a point on the 15th coordinate to the right and seven tenths of the space between the 10th & 11th horizontal coordinates on sheet #2526 of the map series "France." Using this system of coordinates, it was relatively simple to locate the position of our units and our neighbors, proposed attack phase lines, locations of headquarters, etc. The area covered by our 4x4-foot map, when assembled, tacked down and covered with the acetate sheet, would be roughly 19 miles across and 19 miles from bottom to top. Extreme care had to be taken when posting the map because the grease pencil tip itself could be a factor since, even when newly sharpened, the pencil made a line that was equivalent to approximately 100 feet on the map.

The map, used to plot battle plans and the first item to be viewed by visitors, was my responsibility. When time permitted, we would also put together a 1:50,000 map which would show a much larger portion of the battlefield.

Another function was the receipt and dissemination of Operations Orders. Each unit operated on the basis of written orders that would detail the objectives, the forces to be used, the enemy dispositions, the operational plan, and the logistical and communications details. When the urgency of the moment required the issuance of verbal orders, they would always be confirmed in writing as soon as possible.

We also kept the journal, which was a log of all events, messages and the like, which flowed through G-3 during the day. We had mimeographed sheets, which were lined and ruled in columns so that the date, time of day, and title of message or event could be noted. Each item was given a serial number to be listed on the master journal page and then filed in folders in order of occurence. We would have to review this material each day to assure that everything was entered and in proper place. In the heat of events this sometimes was not as easy as it may sound.

The above were our normal activities. I usually stayed up until after the dissemination of the Situation Report and just before dawn I would wake up Colonel Weinecke for the start of his day. Then I would get a few hours sleep, somewhere in a ditch or cellar. I had a very good working relationship with Weinecke, who I found to be very well organized, efficient and even-keeled, under sometimes extreme pressure. As mentioned earlier, Lange and I also were together most of the time, working as a team. For the rest of Headquarters, there was always a G-2 detachment, led by Spotswood, where we were. Most of the rest of Headquarters we never saw, or did so only fleetingly.

Sometime during the first week or so came the word that Jungclas had died, having been in a German Aid Station that was hit by our bombs or artillery. Again, I did not know the source of the news, which I thought could have been a rumor, but it turned out to be all too true. I wanted to treat it as a rumor mainly, I suppose, because he had been standing in for me. Many years later, in 1970, on my first trip back to Normandy, I looked up the register of the men buried in the magnificent cemetery on top of Omaha Beach and his name was on the list. I visited the grave and his date of death is chiseled on the cross above his grave as June 15th, 1944. So, as it turned out, the foul-up that occurred when I was away from the group in southern England just before D-Day probably saved my life. Apparently his glider landed not too far beyond the beaches and amidst some German forces and he was immediately captured in either a wounded or injured condition.

We did not talk too much about Jungclas, because we didn't know the details. But war made death a very real part of life and there wasn't time for mourning. In his case, we could only hope that the news wasn't so. I had developed a method of handling things that could be called denial. Because Junky's death was difficult to accept, it was easier to convince myself that it wasn't so. I did a lot of similar thinking;

for example, the bombing "was worse over there (the next field) than here," or "the flak doesn't seem to be coming close." I also sometimes would be experiencing something and also looking at myself experiencing whatever it was at the same time. If faced with a difficult 8-hour stretch from, say, midnight to 8 A.M., I would divide it in half and aim for 4 A.M., then divide once again to 2 A.M. Then, if I made it to 2 A.M., the mental process would say, "You're halfway home to the first objective—if you can get through half, the rest is downhill." Similar thinking would take over at 4 A.M. relative to arriving at 8 A.M. This internalizing carried me a good bit of the way.

Because of the loss of Jungclas, and Richard leaving us just before D-Day and Pritikin being sick, we were quite undermanned. Sgt. Leonard, from the Airborne Brigade, was with us for a while but he went to either the 507th or 508th after a few days. Even so, we did, from time to time, manage to get a few hours "off." On one such occasion, Wilhelm and I borrowed a jeep and headed for the beaches where we heard there were portable showers set up and we would be able to get clean uniforms. All uniforms worn in the initial landings were impregnated with a chemical that would resist penetration from an attack by gas. Everything was sticky and became stiff and really smelly after a few days, and we couldn't wait to change into clean clothes. We were still in the Ste. Mere Eglise area near our original CP when we made our way down to the beach.

Once there we could see why we were going to win the war. It was only five days or so after the invasion and the beach was crawling with men and equipment. And what equipment! Giant bulldozers, cranes, earth-moving shovels and even locomotives for the French railroad system. This was besides the long rows of tanks, half-tracks, guns and trucks. And the men were streaming in on landing craft from the immense fleet still anchored off the Norman coast. We found the shower unit, called "Fumigation and Bath," and took advantage of the ability to luxuriate (for three minutes) in hot water and soap. Then we picked up clean uniforms and dumped our stinky ones without regret, after removing the various insignia, which would be sewed on the new uniform when possible.

On an earlier afternoon, Wilhelm and I picked ourselves up for a jaunt into Ste. Mere Eglise, passing along the way I had come the morning of D-Day and locating the field in which I had landed. The glider was still there, a grotesque wreck, leading us to wonder how anyone had survived. I had my camera with me and we took eight pictures (the limit of a Brownie roll), including "my" glider and others. Coming into Ste. Mere there was a peculiarly shaped narrow building on which half a glider had come to rest on a shed which protruded from the lower section of the building. In a small garden alongside the house, vegetables were being grown. We helped ourselves to some green onions, which we would use later to spice up our rations. The gardener, a typical red-cheeked Norman in the usual blue work clothes and boots, a rather large man, came out and gave us a huge welcome and insisted we join him in a drink of Calvados, the local firewater. This, of course, we did.

In 1970, when I came back to Ste. Mere, I stopped in the pharmacy of Henri Renaud, who was the son of the wartime mayor and was active in the affairs of the 82d Division Association. I told him of my objective to try to find various landmarks and showed him the pictures of the odd house and the field in which I landed. He immediately took off his pharmacist's white coat and led us (Alice and I) to the odd-shaped house. Miraculously, the garden was replanted and, it being almost the same time of year, was in the same level of growth. It seemed that the same beanpoles were in use. But the best part was that the same red-cheeked Norman in seemingly the same blue uniform and boots was still there and, once again, insisted on us joining him in a glass of Calvados!

By the time the campaign had ended we, as individuals and as a group, had become battle-wise veterans. We knew the rigors and dangers of the field and had become adept at handling our affairs and persons in the midst of almost constant danger. At the same time, what we went through in no way could be compared to the hell of the rifleman in the front line. But we had learned to do what was expected of us and we did it well.

We were relieved by the 8th Infantry Division above La Haye du Puits and settled into a rest area for a couple of days before embarking over the beach for England. I was given the assignment by Wienecke (who by now was Acting Chief of Staff) to draw up a flow-of-battle map which would accompany a text he was having written.

This was done by assigning colors to the various regiments and following their movements by directional arrows in the assigned colors. Thus we were able to broadly recreate the battle for Normandy (our part) on one oversized sheet. The accompanying text was hand-lettered by Floyd Cravath of G-2, who was excellent at that skill. This became our After Action Report. As the battle in France progressed, these reports by various formations became more and more elaborate as competition set in as to who could be the most innovative in their design and execution. (At some point, someone should have called a halt to the excesses.) Colonel Rusk, taking advantage of Wienecke being spread between two offices, signed the report as the Official, although this was a G-3 production. (Leading us to ask—would there ever be an end to this guy?)

A truck pulled up in our area and dumped off a load of new jump boots and we each rummaged through the pile to find a pair in the right size. Jump boots were, of course, a prize possession and delineated Airborne from the rest of the army.

Dorant and I were summoned, the evening before we left France, to Ridgway's tent, in front of which he sat with Wienecke. They were both relaxed. Ridgway was smiling (for once) and said something like, "You men did a magnificent job. You should be proud." Of course, that put us on cloud nine.

The next day we trucked and marched back to the beaches, passing those who were on their way to battle for the first time and who looked at us with querulous envy. We left from Omaha Beach, which had been so hotly contested on D-Day, and walked down the very bluffs and beaches where so many men of the 1st and 29th Divisions had fallen. (We did not know then the severity of those losses.)

We were a relaxed and quietly exuberant lot (slightly fearful of an air attack on the beach while we were there) and loaded in the afternoon onto an empty LST, which was on its way back to Southampton in England. There were no sleeping accommodations but we gratefully made ourselves comfortable on the sheet steel deck, anticipating once again the pleasures of being served Navy food. The crossing to Southampton was overnight and we debarked directly onto trains with our pockets bulging with oranges (!) and other delicacies. We were quite conscious of everybody staring at us as veterans leaving the battle—everyone else was headed for it. We were slightly unkempt and dressed in various forms of uniform, so were quite noticeable.

We unloaded what was left of the oranges quickly when we found ourselves in a station along the way to Leicester at rest alongside a train full of English children. We knew that perhaps these kids had never seen an orange, since Britain had been at war for five years, so we reached across the narrow area between our trains and gave the exotic fruit to those joyful children, who didn't seem to know what to do with them. I'm sure they found out, but we never witnessed the event as our train jerked to a start and we were on our way again.

The train pulled into a siding in Leicester and we could see our familiar trucks lined up for us, and (shades of my first day in Ft. Bragg) we noticed our band, drawn up in formation, which immediately launched into "The All-American Soldier," giving us all goose bumps and an extra spring to our weary bodies. General Gavin was there, all spruced up in class-A uniform, and, as has been noted earlier, cut a handsome figure indeed. We were, in a sense, home, having lived in Leicester for some months and gotten to know many of its people. It was a great day, made better as the people in the streets cheered us as we rode by in our somewhat bedraggled shape—on our way to some rest and rehabilitation, known in the Army as R&R.

The very next day came notification that I had received a promotion to Staff Sergeant (Wilhelm also was promoted to my now vacated spot on the Table of Organization). And a day later, orders were issued awarding me the Bronze Star, mentioning, among other things, the lonely walk I took along the railroad tracks outside of Ste. Mere Eglise.

We were slated to get furloughs, which would be done in two groups. I had found out through reading the Secret ETO Station List that my brother Milton's division, the 80th, had arrived in England and was stationed in the Manchester area. I called him by telephone (which was hooked up to the English system), not realizing that this would cause him to be accused of a breach of security. That was eventually smoothed out. I decided to visit him on my furlough. At one point before I left, Ridgway, now seeming in a mellow mood, asked me what I was planning. I told him about going to the 80th and he remarked it was a good outfit under the command of a good general,

McBride. The 80th later was teamed with the 4th Armored in Patton's Third Army and gave an exceptional account of itself.

And so ended our part of the Normandy saga. Our small band at Headquarters had done well. Now we were ready to regroup and take on the next assignment.

16

HOLLAND

I recall a late afternoon, shortly after our return from Normandy, when Dorant and I strutted into downtown Leicester, cleaned up, shaved and in pressed uniforms, feeling on top of the world. We were basking in a euphoria based on the flush of victory, relief to have survived battle in one piece, a return to civilization, and proud to be part of our Division

This was not to last for long. We shortly would become involved in a series of plans that kept changing as soon as they could be devised, because the fluidity of the front lines in France made plans obsolete before they would become solidified.

But first we were off on furloughs. I had looked up the whereabouts of the 80th Division, then located somewhere on the outskirts of Manchester, and made my way over there, mainly by train but then hitchhiking my way, not knowing exactly where they were. I finally was able to flag down a jeep manned, fortunately, by some MP's of the 80th. They looked at me oddly, but listened to my story of trying to find Co. B of the 319th Infantry. Their Division had only been overseas for a couple of weeks and the MP's were very security conscious, having had the no-no's drummed into them.

They deposited me at the 319th, I found my way to Co. B, and had a reunion with Milton. Now, of course, the relations were reversed. No longer the younger brother who entered the Army as a recruit almost two full years after he had, I was now the veteran with three full campaigns behind me before his outfit had even approached the battlefield. I answered questions as best I could, trying mainly to allay the fears that I knew all of his Company had. I spoke for a while with the Company commander, discussing weapons, both ours and the enemy's. I also had to reassure the Intelligence guys of the 319th that I came by the station listing legitimately, and that I found them not through any lapse of discipline by Milton.

I stayed with the 319th overnight and then helped Milton secure an overnight pass so that we could spend a night in Manchester, where we were able to get a passable meal and have a few beers in a pub. We also had a memorable picture taken at a commercial photographer that happily turned out OK. I was trying to get information from him about home and family—not too much was forthcoming.

It was ships passing in the night. The next morning, Milt took off to find his way back to his outfit and I went in the other direction, stopping off in Birmingham, where I spent a day with Mabel and Harold Goldman in their family's home. I had the films I took in Normandy developed as soon as I came back to Leicester from France and I had the prints with me. Somehow, taking a camera along was something that would not be done by an English soldier unless specifically authorized, and there was some surprise that I was able to do so. Anyway, everyone was impressed by the prints which showed, most particularly, the damage done to the gliders in the initial landings.

"Back at the office" things were happening. Ridgway was leaving us to take over the XVIII Airborne Corps, and he was taking all his staff with him except Weinecke, who was promoted to full colonel and was to be the new Chief of Staff. Gavin was taking over the 82d from Ridgway and bringing most of the 505th regimental staff to join him.

I was going to miss Weinecke, with whom I had worked so closely in Normandy and whom we all found to be an excellent officer. I came of age as a soldier under his command. Actually, in Normandy he had two jobs, G-3 and Chief of Staff, because he had to take over from Eaton who was injured (or wounded) and evacuated. Colonel Emory Adams had taken over from Weinecke briefly as G-3, but only served for a few days when he became ill, so Weinecke served both functions almost for the whole campaign. But all was not lost.

Coming in as G-3 was Jack Norton, to whom I had been assigned in Sicily with the Pathfinder experimental group. We soon found that we had a winner. A West Pointer, he lived and breathed Army and, even though a relative youngster, his training had generated a professional approach to his job which was augmented by his native abilities and personality. Throughout the succeeding months, during which I came to know him well, I was always impressed with the analytical way he approached each problem, with his decisiveness in developing and executing his plans, and his ever-present good cheer. From the day he took over until the end of the war, I never saw him lose his cool. He never dressed anyone down, yet I think we had the most smoothly functioning section in our headquarters. On the other side, he wrote me forty years later that when he first took over from Weinecke, the Colonel had told him I was "tops" and that I had worked out as predicted.

We also fleshed out the enlisted complement. We were Dorant, myself, Lange, Wilhelm, Rohr and Pritikin (coming back after his illness). Normandy had shown that we needed more men, particularly when we were on the move with more than one Command Post in operation. Two young privates, Gilbertson and DeTomasso, had come to us through the normal replacement process. As time passed, they both became good additions. Later, Bulleit, a parachutist with the rank of Corporal, joined us. Then in walked Hidalgo, also a parachutist, transferred to us carrying the rank of Master Sergeant! We never found out the details of where he came from and why, but we soon came to really like the guy—he was like our mascot, even though he had none of the background necessary for G-3.

Hidalgo was of Mexican heritage and lived in the Texas border town of Del Rio. We came to love him and his broken English, his tales of amorous adventures, and the simple way he approached life and soldiering. It was impossible to imagine him without his smile and pleasant demeanor. Unfortunately for him, he came to us with the rank of Master Sergeant—there was only one such rank permissible in our Section and he was subsequently reduced in rank to corporal, which he accepted with his usual good humor.

Up till this point our division headquarters had been a glider outfit, but the coming of Gavin and his staff changed that around completely, as all the members of it coming from the 505th were parachutists. There always had been some unpublicized finger pointing at "them," meaning the gliderborne guys in headquarters, and being one of "them" carried some stigma of second-class citizenship.

As it was at the time, the only enlisted parachutists in our group were Hidalgo and Bulleit. Bulleit was a crackerjack typist but Hidalgo, as noted, was completely new to our operation and it was soon discovered had many shortcomings as an Operations Sergeant.

We all obviously at one point or other had considered the ramifications of taking jump training. A school had been conducted in Africa and a number of men had volunteered and gone through a hastily organized course there. When we first entered the Army, even though we were immediately assigned to the 82d, the idea of volunteering for jump school didn't even enter our minds, it seemed so foreign to us. I had even given a confident promise to Alice that I wouldn't ever volunteer. It didn't take much soul searching at the time, it was so obvious. However, a lot of water had gone under the bridge in the ensuing two years. The British glider operation in Sicily had been disastrous with enormous casualties. From my own observation in Normandy, the glider landings were far more dangerous and had a higher percentage of casualties than the parachute landings. I knew that I would rather come in by parachute—it was safer. By now I was a veteran soldier; I had been through the mill and didn't stand in awe of things as I did in the fall of 1942. I didn't like to back out on a promise to Alice but that promise had been made without benefit of the knowledge I now had.

So when Norton raised the question, "Who will be in the jump echelon in the next operation?" Willis Lange and I both answered in the affirmative, and were then enrolled in a hastily organized two-week school to be conducted within the division area. Spotswood and White of G-2 and Moore of G-4 also volunteered. The die had been cast.

John White, one of the volunteers, was southern born, a loner, and distinguished himself only on those occasions when he would get drunk and go around picking fights until he found someone who would oblige. He seemingly found some kind of release in these engagements. Jim Spotswood found, however, that John, when sober was his best man.

We were a group of about 40 officers and men and started the training in a mock-up body of a C-47 plane. We were taught first how to put on the parachutes (main and reserve), the technique of hooking up the static line (which opened the chute after one left the plane), how to shuffle up to the door of the plane and then exit, arms folded around the reserve parachute in front of the body, with a turn after exiting to face the rear.

Then we went to harness drill, in which we were suspended by the parachute risers from higher supports, and we were drilled in how to handle the risers so as to maneuver the parachute during descent.

We also did jumping and landing drills from a six-foot platform in which we were instructed in the methods of tumbling on hitting the ground from any angle (front, rear or side). The idea was to hit softly, collapse in the direction of one's motion, tumble to minimize the impact, and to gain control of one's body prior to getting out of the parachute harness. The parachutes had now been fitted with quick-release gizmos, which released the harness after a well placed blow with one's fist or palm.

We did all that and also went through the obligatory calisthenics and body building drills, running, push-ups, etc. All of this was done in one concentrated week and brought us to the stage of our first jump. In the meantime, we would go back each day, usually about time for evening chow, enter the mess hall trying to hide our smug grins, noting the glances being shot our way—the celebrities of the moment. Everything became a little more intense as the day approached.

And approach it did. By now we were all carried along by group psychology—there would be no turning back, no matter how sweaty, nervous and downright scared we might be. We nervously endured the truck ride to the airfield where on the tarmac there were a few C-47's lined up. The procedure was that the plane would take off, circle around a while, and then one man would jump, to be followed by another circling of the field, another jump, etc., until the entire "stick" had jumped. The door was open and the jumpmaster stood next to it and shouted instructions relating to hooking up, getting to the door, standing in the door, observing the red light (ready) and watching for the green light (go). As I was hoping for an honorable way out of all this, we were moving closer to the event. The jump was to be from about 1,500 feet. I was to be the second man out (thank my stars I wasn't the last) and watched as the first man got up, shuffled to the door after hooking up the static line, and stood in it on the order of the jumpmaster. He then disappeared out the door when the green light came on.

Now it's my turn. I willed myself to my feet, knees really like rubber, hooked up and hesitantly advanced to the door. The plane was completing its circle and heading back to the drop zone area. The jumpmaster beckoned for me to come closer to the door and then invited me to look out as he pointed to the approaching field where one could see panels laid out for recognition purposes. I barely looked out and weakly nodded my head. Then there was the order to "Stand in the Door," which meant inching one's way up to the sill of the door, put one hand on each door frame, prepared to push out. And then, inevitably, "GO," and I flung myself out (probably barely missing the door frame), turned to the rear with my arms folded over the reserve chute on my belly, counted 1,000, 2,000, 3,000 and, lo, just as they said, the main chute opened with a series of jerks felt throughout my entire body. Then I was suspended in the air, seemingly not moving at all, except for some gentle swaying.

I reached above my head, reassuringly found the risers and grasped them and felt a wave of almost unbelievable elation. But, to the business at hand. I still had to land. Floating through the air was just that — there was no wind so it was a gentle descent, and after a few seconds it did seem that the ground was getting closer and that I was coming in on the proper direction. Then suddenly, the ground started rushing up to me and, bang, I landed in a crumpled mess, collapsed the air out of the chute as soon as I could, righted myself on my feet and disengaged myself from the harness. I thought I had done just fine but an observer on the ground said I was bicycling with my feet as I approached the ground (a no-no) and that I had really hit the ground in as ungraceful a manner as possible. Well, nothing could have been said that would have made me feel bad at that moment. I had done it! This was the ultimate victory over fear. We rode back to camp like heroes ready to answer all the questions that we knew would be thrown at us.

The following day we jumped in a stick, that is all men going out in a group, one after the other, which called for more discipline than individually jumping. Getting out the door quickly was a survivor technique, because the faster the group left the door the closer together they would be as they reached the ground, obviously better for tactical reasons.

On the third day we took two jumps, one in the morning, the other in the afternoon. On the second of these jumps, I reached up for the risers after the chute opened and they weren't there! Reason and panic battled—I knew I wasn't dropping like a stone so I had to be suspended from the chute. I twisted back and craned my neck so that I could look up (complicated by the presence of my helmet), and noticed that the risers instead of coming to my back as four individual lines, were twisted in a rope-like manner. What must have happened was that my exit position had been just right for the blast from the propellers to catch me and start to turn me rapidly as the chute was opening. I debated as to whether to open the reserve chute but noticed that I wasn't descending any faster than the others so I refrained from that and then became aware that the rope of the risers was slowly unwinding and I was accordingly twisting in the air, ever more rapidly. When it had completely unraveled, it started twisting in the other direction. I was able to stop this somewhat by reaching up, grabbing the risers and attempting to stabilize them. By the time I reached the ground I wasn't circling anymore but was oscillating rather wildly and hit the ground with my feet, then head, then back—unhurt!

The final jump was at night with limited visibility, and less chance of being able to sight and move toward a safe-appearing spot. There were, however some red light markers on the field we were to land on and, surprisingly, the jump in the dark seemed to go much easier than the earlier daylight ones. So much for expectations. On the ground after this fifth and last jump I became aware that I had lost my helmet, probably scraped off as the chute opened. Someone was shouting my name, so I answered and it turned out to be Colonel Norton, who gave me a big greeting on the ground, which I gratefully accepted in my hyper-ventilated state. It was a great moment. I felt, as did the others in the same boat, that I had arrived, met the challenge and, in a sense, became legitimately a member of the 82d Airborne Division.

There was a small ceremony in our G-3 hut the next morning when Lange and I were given our parachute wings. We basked in the attention and glory for a couple of days, but then it was on to the next step.

Things were happening so rapidly in France that there were hopes abounding that the war would soon be over. Advances were being made daily by our First and Third Armies and, finally, by the British as well, who were advancing rapidly through Belgium and approaching Holland. Those were heady days.

As noted earlier, we worked on a series of potential operations where we would be used to drop in advance of our armies, but by the time these plans developed, the quickness of the advances out-distanced the objectives and made the operations unnecessary.

Meantime, the vital strategic debate was going on at the highest levels as to where the Allies would make their main effort for the final defeat of Germany. As the front lines began to out-distance supplies that were still trucked in over the original beaches and sped to the advancing armies, the seemingly never-ending supply stream finally began to dry up.

In the event, the British proposals were accepted by Eisenhower and plans were made for a massive assault to the north on the British Second Army front which would end up with successive crossings of rivers and canals that would put the British with nothing but open plains between them and the heart of Germany. As part of the plan, the newly formed Allied Airborne Army would be dropped along the route with the mission of securing the various river crossings. The British 1st Airborne and our 82d and 101st Divisions would be used, along with the Polish Parachute Brigade, which had been thirsting for action since the war had begun.

We were given the middle area with the major crossings of the Maas River at Grave and the Waal River at Nijmegen as our major objectives. Planning began in earnest. Once again we were in and out of the War Room, working feverishly to get the plans and orders in shape. The Airborne forces on the ground would be commanded by Lt. General Browning (British) with Ridgway sadly having no role, even though the majority of the forces were American.

There was no way an operation of this magnitude could be staged without intricate planning and, in the precious couple of weeks it took, the Germans managed to collect stragglers from here and there and get them into some form of defensive stance now that the borders of their country were about to be breached. Nijmegen, our main objective, bordered Germany with the bridges to be assaulted being within several miles of the border. We received Intelligence Reports that there was a concentration of German armor in the Reichswald (a wooded area over the border in Germany), but they were discounted as probably being exaggerated or completely untrue. Most talk was about an electrifying victory, one that would bring the end of the war within sight.

Once again I stayed at our headquarters (this time in Leicester) until the last moment while almost everybody had been securely sealed in at the departing airports. However, it was impossible to keep complete secrecy because the war-wise British populace recognized the unusual activities and knew something was up. On that Sunday morning, Dorant and I left Leicester armed to the teeth with weapons, ammunition, grenades, etc., and thought it would be fun to stop our jeep at an open store to buy newspapers. (It sounds outlandish as I write it, but we did.) The locals in the store noticed our warlike appearance, gave us lots of noncommittal glances, but no one said anything.

It was a glorious Sunday in September and the great armada took off in a never-ending stream that stretched from airfields all over Britain. We were escorted by swarms of fighter planes, saw nary a German one, and were able to see civilians on the roofs of their houses waving us on. It was kind of like a victory march. We were to land outside of Groesbeek, which, in turn, was outside of Nijmegen, astride the German border. This operation was in daylight, the first time that had been done and the results in precision and reduced casualties were marked.

This time I was with men from my own outfit and would link up with the gliderborne jeeps and trailers on the same drop zone we were using. The difference between the cliffhanging enormity of the event in Normandy with this seemingly Sunday afternoon picnic ride to Holland was startling. Daylight made a tremendous difference. The drop zone turned out to be a sugar beet field, which was quite soft and easy to land on. Even so, there were problems, particularly with some of the gliders. There had been little or no German resistance along the route, except some antiaircraft fire, which exacted a small toll.

We hastily assembled in a wooded area alongside the sugar beet fields and, this time the various units for the most part were able to assemble and begin execution of their missions without delay. The huge bridge at Grave was taken almost immediately, but a major battle was developing in the outskirts of Nijmegen and near the approaches to the Nijmegen bridges (one railroad and one road traffic). We set up our Command Post in a wooded area near some railroad tracks.

That first evening we learned that one of our jeep drivers, Hostler, and one of the G-2 men, Cravath, had been killed in crashed glider landings. Good-hearted Strother, a particular friend of Cravath, was in tears. It seems cold of us now but there was not much else to do but to continue "as we were." Some years later, an honor roll of those who died was being assembled at the Nijmegen Museum of the Battle, and I saw to it that Hostler and Cravath were suitably listed.

The Dutch people were particularly welcoming, greeting the soldiers with armloads of apples and other goodies. They had to learn (sadly, in some cases) that the war was not over simply because we were there, but there were long days ahead.

An odd thing that happened early on in the campaign was the presence of German jet fighters over the battlefield. They were strange in the noise they made—a whisper rather than a roar—and in the difficulty of seeing them because their speed was so much greater than conventional aircraft. They were usually out of sight by the time we looked up to see them. Fortunately for our side, they were in their infancy, not too many of them were in the sky, and they were basically ineffective in the battle.

A couple of days after the start of the campaign there was an exceedingly heavy rainstorm which held up reinforcement by the Polish Brigade at Arnhem. The rain also affected the resupply missions which were dropped from low-flying bombers. Mainly missing their targets, most of the materials were probably recovered by the Germans.

And we were always reminded, mainly through our rations, that we had been attached to the British Army for this operation. Their rations included an instant tea concentrate that included milk and sugar—all one had to do was add water. We kind of got used to it and it wasn't bad. They also had a liquor ration! With this ration there was a rigid structure of what each rank (officer and enlisted man) received, ranging from a couple of beers for a private to bottles of whiskey for the higher ranks. We got a little more than our share because I always made sure we included the various liaison officers and their drivers on our list, even though they were drawing rations from their own out-fits. This we considered to be legitimate stealing. All in all the rations, especially the liquor, weren't too bad. One of the little by-plays had to do with a wicker-enclosed bottle of gin belonging to Captain Graham that disappeared. He remembered this in correspondence we had forty years after the war.

We also caught on quickly to the British way of heating water or food, which came, we were told, from their experiences in the North African desert. One of the staples of their rations were biscuits which came in large tin containers about 10 inches square and about a foot high. The trick was to remove the top of the can completely, fill it about half full of sand, pour some gasoline into it, add a match and, *voila!*, a perfect stove for heating your soup, shaving water, or what-ever. You could get a nice blaze for about five minutes or so, and stir it up with a stick or bayonet for a couple of more minutes after the ini-tial flame died down. Then you had to let it die out. Adding gasoline while it was burning was an absolute no-no, as we saw one day when one guy was pouring some gas out of a 5-gallon can onto a dying fire, which then leapt into immediate tongues of flame which scattered the GI's in the area. Fortunately, no one was injured.

The CP was located in a triangular-shaped wooded area bordering on St. Anna Straat, a road leading into Nijmegen. We dug our indi-vidual holes on the other side of a dirt road from the CP and did so with particular vigor after we began to be bombarded by heavy artillery each afternoon and evening, the attack lasting for about two weeks. I dug an L-shaped hole for myself about 2 feet wide and 4 feet deep, with enough length to accommodate my body without extend-ing into the bottom of the "L". I cut down some small trees with a borrowed axe and crossed the open top of the hole with small logs, covering them with dirt from the hole which was placed in plastic gas-protective bags and then repeated the process, making a very secure den. Over the course of time, I cut a couple of shelves into the dirt and constructed a step coming into the L from the outside. It was fairly homey.

Willis Lange dug a hole near mine. One night we were under a particularly heavy attack with the shrapnel whistling through the woods and debris falling all around. After each salvo, Willis would holler "Are you OK, Leonard?" For some reason, his shouting to me was comical and I was alternating between cringing from the shells and laughing from Willis' shouts.

We rapidly established our working quarters and had a most efficient Operations Section going. Because we were not split up into advance and rear we had adequate personnel and settled down to a steady routine. I was on duty most of the days and pitched in occasionally at night when the Situation Report went out. I was responsible for the upkeep of the map, which would reflect every movement of our troops, show patrolling areas, offensive and defensive positions, etc. There is an often duplicated picture of General Gavin briefing General Dempsey, Commander of the British Second Army, in our CP and the map he is pointing to is my Operations map.

Some of us became acquainted with the families living on the other side of St. Anna Straat. One of them was the van Hoorns, who were a relatively young couple with three young children. After we got to know them better, I often spent the early evening in their living room listening to the BBC and having tea (!) while the occasional aircraft would drop some bombs in the area. They were sleeping in the cellar with the children and, on occasion, Mike (last name forgotten), a big MP, and I would sack out with our clothes and boots on using their comfortable bed. *C'est la guerre!*

In 1984 we took a tour with the C-47 Club, observing the 40th Anniversary of D-Day with a visit to Ste. Mere Eglise, Nijmegen and the Belgian battlefields. In Nijmegen we were guests of the Wiendels family and, when I told them of my experiences in Dekker Wald, Johan stepped up to try and locate the wooded area and the van Hoorns. Our first efforts were unsuccessful but he persisted and ultimately Johan informed me in an excited manner that he had located where the van Hoorns had lived. They had moved, but their neighbors begged Johan to bring us around, which he did. The reason, it turned out, that we didn't recognize the house earlier was that post-war construction had cut a road one door down from the house and, because of that the street front was different and I was disoriented. Anyway, we came to see the neighbors, who were delighted and very happy to see me. Their young grandson came forward manfully and said, "Thank you for making us free" (in English). It was very affecting.

Then Johan came with us across the street into the wood, across the triangular area and the dirt road into the area in which we had dug those impressive holes. And just where I thought they would be, there they were! The sides had collapsed somewhat, but there were still rotted timbers across the top. I am still amazed they were there. We took pictures and then found out why the area was relatively untouched— it was owned by the city and was over the wells from which the city's water supply was drawn, therefore the plot was never used or built upon.

The differences between the Normandy and Holland campaigns were marked. All the important events were played out in a few days in Holland, during which the Division was beleaguered on all sides and an unbelievably daring crossing of the Rhine by the 504th in canvas boats was accomplished as part of the assault which took the bridges across the Waal River.

Forty years later, in 1984, I stood on the far bank of the river (where the enemy had been) marveling at the absolute courage of the men of the 504th who launched canvas boats and crossed the broad river in the face of German machine gun fire, with only a drifting smoke barrage for cover. Absolutely amazing! And those intrepid soldiers who survived the crossing then made a mad dash for the north end of the road bridge.

In the meantime the 505th, which had been held up by withering fire in its block-by-block, house-by-house attack to the south end of the bridge, capped a decimating battle and, along with tanks from the British Guards Armored Division, finally reached the bridge at the same time the 504th appeared at the north end.

Heroes all!

But there were delays by the British XXX Corps, which had the job of dashing up the road from the Belgian border and continuing to Arnhem. By the time they got across the Nijmegen Bridge in our area the British 1st Airborne in Arnhem to the north had been practically wiped out of existence. There were recriminations against the British armor in that they did not immediately drive toward Arnhem after the bridge at Nijmegen was ours, but instead took time out "for tea" and called off the day's activities just north of the bridge. This infuriated the commander of the 504th, Colonel Tucker, and the rest of our command. A weak attempt by the British on the next day to move up the road was repulsed, resulting in the decision to remove the remnants of the British Airborne from Arnhem.

Although it was not realized and accepted as such at the time, this noble adventure to the north, Montgomery's baby, turned out to be a failure. The massive effort, which included diverting a huge part of the Allied supply channel, brought the British Army to the German/ Dutch border in September, at which point they still remained the following April. The British 1st Airborne Division had ceased to exist. The Polish Brigade, which was not part of the initial assault because of the limitations of the airlift, was piecemealed into the battle and was not effective.

After the first 10 days of the battle, it became a static affair with most of the activity being confined to patrolling, occasional raids, artillery duels and forays by aircraft on both sides. As noted earlier, we settled in a wooded area south of the center of Nijmegen, using tents for our operating HQ with some trenches and foxholes nearby for cover. At some point we also had a large underground war room constructed that was like a page out of a World War I movie.

It was in this bunker, one afternoon, that I was reading mail that had just been delivered, and there was a letter from my half-brother, Herbert, mentioning that Milton had been wounded and assuming I knew about it. What a shock! I had just seen him a few weeks earlier. My mental process of minimizing things immediately came into play and it went something like, "It's probably not too bad, most wounds aren't, and, also, at least for the time being he's out of harm's way and he wasn't killed." But it was a sobering shock indeed. I tried to imagine the effect of the news on the family back home and I wrote to Pop trying to help him through the bad news. I also mentally replayed versions of the contrast between his service and mine, his being so much longer, but his exposure to the enemy so much shorter, etc., etc. It was a relief to know that he was alive and probably free from danger for the rest of the war.

A project had been started of interviewing a representative of each plane or glider load to determine where each had landed, the condition of the landing, lists of casualties, etc. This was to be statistically compiled in a series of charts and also represented on maps with each plane's entry point shown as a dot on a 1:25,000 Map. It was a large project and was conducted by each battalion and regiment separately and then submitted to us at G-3. I made up the maps.

Simultaneously, a narrative was being developed by Colonel Norton of the entire operation and this was to be accompanied by a series of maps and sketches. The colonel and I established ourselves in a schoolhouse not too far from Dekker Wald and worked intensively for a couple of weeks on the project. The largely static battle continued and my best memory of it was coming back from the schoolhouse at the end of a day and evening, walking across several fields to the accompaniment of Screaming Meemies (or Nebelwerfers, to give them their German name). They were a type of rocket mortar, consisting of a series of tubes which would eject their projectiles along with a series of high-pitched groans or whistles which were very intimidating. It all had to do with the noise.

In the meantime the G-3 routine continued. Since we had a full crew in one location, the workload was easily handled. However, war was getting to Dorant. We were under attack almost nightly and Chester was obviously under a strain. Always one to look for some diversion, he had gotten into the routine of scouting about each evening, with some buddies and an accessible jeep, for alcohol in any form. Strangely enough, even with the war going on it was available, and Chester ended up many an evening in an alcoholic haze which probably was an answer to whatever demons he was battling. The rest of us covered for him, as we knew he would do for us.

When the job of the after-action report, with accompanying maps and charts was ready, I was given the assignment of taking it to 8th Air Force Headquarters at High Wycombe, north of London, where there was a printing plant, to get the job into print. I was issued the necessary orders, told to report to 1st Allied Airborne Army Headquarters initially and take it from there. The first step was to get back to England and it was suggested I get to an Air Force installation outside of Brussels and hitchhike to England. So we carefully packed up the maps, charts and written material and I hastily threw some personal things together, left my other stuff in the care of Lange and the rest, and off I went.

17

SIDE TRIP TO ENGLAND

So I was off on another Odyssey. Starting with the advance party from Camp Edwards to Staten Island before shipping out to Africa, I had been tapped for the initial party into Sicily, joined the special radar-Pathfinding group in Sicily, picked up the manifests of the tail groups leaving that island, wended my way back to Naples solo (with driver), been on the advance detachment from Ireland to England, and now was going back to England on detached service from the Continent with the task of reproducing the records of the Holland invasion.

Somewhere along the line our A-bags, which included changes of clothing, had been brought up, so I was able to dig up a relatively clean uniform and some underwear and socks. I put on the O.D.'s, stuffed some other items and plenty of cigarettes in a musette bag, and was ready to go, leaving my green combat suit and helmet in the care of others. The written material made a small 8-1/2 x 11-size package and the map material was rolled up and placed in two metal map tubes.

Someone had suggested that a lift could be obtained at an Air Corps installation outside of Brussels and off I went, carrying the good wishes and admonishments of all, with a redheaded driver whose name was Daly. Brussels was a couple of hours away by jeep on roads that were completely controlled by us (we and the British). We would have to feel our way around because we didn't know the precise location of the airfield. So we found our way to Brussels and, on a whim, stopped in at a civilian barbershop to have our hair cut. (Why not?)

While in the chair, I sensed the barber getting nervous every time there was the distant sound of an airplane engine. Odd, I thought, because at that time planes were in the air all over the place, all the time, close and far. The barber kept clipping away, and my red-headed friend was being attended to in a neighboring chair, when the sound of a plane entered the space, growing slightly louder. The barbers became more attentive when, suddenly, the sound broke off and everybody in the shop except my friend and I dove for the floor. A couple of seconds later, there was the force and sound of a huge explosion that rattled the windows and shop. It was a buzz bomb—the German V-1 weapon. It was my first experience with that baby, though it was something the people of London, Brussels and Antwerp had been bombarded with for months. (Although at this time the attack on London was being carried out mainly by V-2 rockets.) Slightly chastened, now with our ears attuned to the sky, we got out of there quickly after the haircuts were over and accosted a succession of Air Corps guys until we found out where the most likely airfield for our purpose would be.

Coming on to the field, I noted the difference between an operational field and the type of installation we were used to housing transport aircraft. I found what looked like an operations hut, walked in and explained my case, finding the usual Air Force informality in effect. I was told, in essence, to be their guest, and if I could find any plane that was going back to England, I could hitch a ride providing I had the plane crew's agreement.

Over on one side there was a Flying Fortress with some work being done on it. I walked over and started talking to some of the men. This plane had been on a bombing run over Germany, had received considerable damage, and had to stop in this interim location to get bandaged up so as to be able to return to England. I noticed that the left wingtip was missing but was assured that the plane could fly in that condition when the other, more important, items were fixed. As a matter of fact, I was told, they were almost ready to finish up and take off.

Now it was only a matter of convincing the pilot to give me a ride, which he kindly agreed to. So I said so-long to Daly and climbed aboard when they were ready. First I had the opportunity to go through the Flying Fort and was impressed with the Spartan nature of the cockpit and fuselage. The main body bristled with .50-caliber machine guns, which were fired through open ports on each side. There was also a tail gunner, a guy suspended in a ball under the plane with dual .50s, a gunner in a ball above and behind the cockpit, and a couple of guns sticking out of the nose. It was a well-armed machine whose solemn task was the delivery of bombs which were located in a bay behind the cockpit and in front of the waist gunners. A couple of the crew had been wounded and were in hospitals in the Brussels area. I was advised that I could fly in the spot reserved for the roof gunner, one of those who had been wounded.

This guy flew standing up with his head in the bubble above the top of the plane and his feet on a round platform just behind the cockpit. I suspect there was an alternate position while out of the combat zone. At any rate, that's how I made the Channel crossing back to England, standing on that platform. When one was in a standing position, grasping the handles of the machine guns, the platform would rotate in response to the pressure developed by the aiming of the guns. In other words, one could turn a complete circle just by moving the handles. It was a giddy experience, kind of like playing with a new toy.

The whole flight, from take-off to landing, seemed to be less than an hour. I drank in the experience of crossing the Channel, seeing those famous white cliffs appear, then the peaceful looking English countryside and, finally, landing on an East Anglia 8th Air Force base. Now, to proceed from there: I had my rifle and musette bag, to which was attached my raincoat. Plus the aforementioned package and map tubes. I also had some English money. My orders directed me to first go to the headquarters of the 1st Allied Airborne Army and secure further written authority which would eventually take me to 8th Air Force Headquarters with a request that I be given assistance in preparing the material for printing and the actual printing thereof.

The guys at the Air Force base were very accommodating. I, coming from the ground war, was as much a curiosity to them as they were to me. I stayed there overnight, was fed a couple of superb (by our standards) meals, and the next day they provided me with a jeep and driver and I was off to the next stop. I checked in with 1st Allied Airborne Army and found, to my surprise, two individuals from the past. One was Colonel Boyd, who was G-3 when I first joined the

Division, now occupying a desk job that he obviously didn't like. I answered many questions for him, as he was thirsty for news of his old outfit. Also there was Sgt. Vines, of D-Day fame, he who had suggested that Colonel Rusk perform an impossible sexual act. Vines looked the same and still carried the same rank. He was obviously pleased to be where he was, but still fuming, when probed, about Rusk, "that SOB." I also filled him in on a lot of scuttlebutt.

And then I was off to XVIIIth Airborne Corps Headquarters, why I don't recall, but I was directed there on the way to High Wycombe. I had the necessary papers directed to 8th Air Force and headed there by train after a brief stopover at Corps Headquarters. I didn't meet any enlisted men at Corps whom I knew but my old nemesis, Colonel Rusk, was there, holding his usual early morning court. Now that he was G-2 of the Corps, he had at least a half dozen subsections under him: Intelligence, Counter-Intelligence, Photo-Reconnaissance, Enemy Order of Battle and the like. Now, knowing Rusk, I knew that he would have daily assignments in all these sections requiring reports. And, sure enough, outside his office there was a line of junior officers, all clutching papers, nervously waiting their turn to go in, make their reports, and be chewed out. What a man! What a disaster!

I got out of there as soon as I could, lest Rusk find out I was there and make some "suggestions." I got a lift to the railroad station and was off to High Wycombe, which is north of London. As I recall, the trip took me through London where I changed trains. It was a little bit of an unusual sight for an American soldier in Britain because I was carrying these packages on public transportation and also my rifle. Now, British soldiers always carried theirs on leave (probably harking back to the early days of the war when invasion may have seemed imminent), but we never did. To the uninitiated, our M-1 rifle looked odd as there was no bolt and the gas chamber below the barrel made the weapon look double-barreled, which it wasn't. Compared to the British Enfield, our Garand M-1 had a heavier, more formidable appearance, and was clearly a better weapon as it fired a full clip of ammunition semi-automatically. I got into some interesting conversations with soldiers and civilians on the train and it was a fun trip.

High Wycombe, finally. Deep into the side of a hill was burrowed the Headquarters installations of the 8th Air Force (our contribution to the round-the-clock bombing of Germany) and also, it seemed, a considerable RAF installation. Streams of uniformed personnel continuously poured in and out of this redoubt, which was the nerve center of the 8th. Above it, on ground level at the top of the hill were the living quarters and less sensitive installations. The town and station were a short walk away.

I reported as directed, was assured that I would receive full cooperation in our project, and was assigned a cot in a tent on top of the hill. Once again, I was a curiosity, practically a celebrity. The men greeted me warmly and we spent evenings drinking beer just off the base. There was a drafting room on the base and I was given a drawing table, supplies, and assurances that my job would be given some priority. I set to work making my sketches and color separations. I spent the better part of a week on that and then turned the work over for printing.

Now I had a few days to myself while that was being done. Somehow I had found out, or was told, where Milton was hospitalized. It was in a Station Hospital in Barnstaple, which is in the west of England, near Wales. Off I went, by now being quite used to being on my own and finding my way around the friendly confines of England.

Milt had been severely wounded, with shrapnel from an exploding shell finding its way into one side of his body from his upper legs to his chest. Some of it had been removed but some was still lodged in his groin and chest areas. It would stay there until he died in 1999, the fragments in his chest, which became surrounded by protective tissue, possibly adding to his difficulties in breathing in his later life. He never smoked a Lucky Strike cigarette again because it was what he was lighting when he was struck. His next memory was regaining consciousness in a field hospital.

This was about two months after he was hit and he was no longer bed-ridden but was still recuperating. After his recovery, he stayed in the same hospital and was trained as a therapist for later patients. Actually he felt some relief in being out of the war, there being no way he would be sent back, and, as we know now, the percentages of being a casualty in an infantry company were extremely high.

We talked and had a few laughs, and I managed to stay overnight with him. My memory is not certain as to whether we were able to leave the hospital grounds, but I was able to report to the family at home that I had seen him, that he was recovering and that he would be safe for the rest of the war.

When I returned to High Wycombe, the job had just about been finished and in a couple of days it was all packed up and I was ready to go. The next step was to go to Leicester, where the 82d still had a rear installation, to hook up with a C-47 that could take me back to the outfit. For this I needed a small truck or van, which was made available by 8th Air Force, and in a few days I was back in the strangely quiet confines of Braunstone Park, which I had left approximately two months earlier.

There was hardly anybody there, kind of like a ghost town. Those who remained were going through slow paces and would not be there for much longer. I found out that the Division had been pulled out of Holland and was now stationed in France in a reserve position. There would be no further returns to England!

What talk there was concerned Swanson. Swanny was a young towhead from somewhere in the midwest and was attached to G-2. He had a choirboy look about him and was happiest when he could cajole someone into having a catch, using a baseball and a couple of gloves he always had handy. He had a stylish motion of throwing and quietly told everyone he was going to be a big-league player. As a lot of guys did, he took up with a young English lass and, prior to Normandy, announced he was going to get married. Well, a big deal was made of this, a party was given, and Swanny was given a special leave of a week as a honeymoon. Consternation set in when he didn't return after the honeymoon, and was not to be found before we went to Normandy, or to Holland either. He was just plain AWOL and couldn't be found. Attempts to reach him through the girl's family were unavailing because no one knew exactly where they were located.

Anyway it turned out that Swanny was in Leicester, living with this girl, whom he had never actually married. He was walking around, not hiding, in his uniform, visiting pubs as he and his girl had done earlier, waiting, most likely, to be found and picked up. This eventually happened and Swanny wound up in the stockade in Braunstone, its only resident. But there are certain guys who always land on their feet. He was so well liked that he got off with a virtual slap on the wrist, forfeiting some "pay and allowances," and never went to military prison.

I had a couple of errands to run for some of the guys, getting stuff from their B Bags, etc., which I did. A flight was being arranged for me and after a few days in Leicester my printed material was loaded on a small truck and we were off to an airfield where there was a C-47 ready to make the run to France. We loaded up, and off we went.

After a flight of a couple of hours we arrived at an airfield near Reims, and I was greeted by a jeep and trailer and Marv Pritikin. Then the shocker: "Chester is dead. He was killed in a jeep accident a couple of nights ago."

We were from different backgrounds and had very little in common except the work we did together, but Chester Dorant had been my good friend in the two years I had known him and I could only speculate that his after-hours carousing and search for alcohol had been his downfall. It was truly a blow, even though it was apparent that I would finally inherit the head of section status.

I was so taken back that I didn't realize that the plane was readying its take-off before I had unloaded my material. I frantically ran in front of the pilot's window waving my arms and got him to cut the engines while Pritikin, the driver and I unloaded the plane.

And that was my welcome back to the 82d.

18

REFITTING IN SISSONNE

From the vantage point of many years later, it is difficult to fathom the whys and wherefores of how we handled death. Today it seems callous, but we didn't mourn, perhaps because death being all around us prompted a sense of avoidance and denial—if one thought too much about it, the obvious conclusion was that one might be next. I had spoken with Cravath about the operation the evening before he died on the landing in Holland, at which time he smiled wanly and asked, "What am I doing here?" I saw Hostler's body laid out next to his crashed glider and moved on. I was acutely aware, when I thought about it, that Jungclas had died perhaps exactly in my place. We didn't talk too much about Dorant. He had died while I was away so I don't know what the on-the-spot reaction had been, but it was probably minimal, even as well liked as he was. In war, sadly, you just moved on.

At the first opportunity, Colonel Norton told me that I was taking over with his full confidence. It was difficult to balance that good news with the bad. I knew I had the support of the men, with the possible exception of Jack Rohr, who was negative about almost everything, not just me. With my agreement, Willis Lange was promoted to my vacated spot, as I was to Dorant's.

We were now established in a French Army barracks that had probably been in existence before World War I. It consisted of rows of long, single-floor cement buildings with crude sanitary facilities, and a two-floor administration building where we had two rooms assigned to G-3 on the upper floor. In a week or two, the tail in England was rolled up and we were all in the same location. We were being re-fitted, getting our personal equipment in order, and being de-loused, etc. I packed up all the stuff I had worn since leaving England for Holland in mid-September (we were now in late November) and it was laundered and treated chemically and delivered back to me in grade-A shape.

I also caught up on all my mail which had been gathering while I was back in England and once again immersed myself in the news from home, picturing Alice's ink-stained fingers as she poured forth her daily stream of letters. Joe was now nearly a year old and, the reports said, progressing beautifully.

The Holland report was well accepted. I had made only one error —on one of the color separations—but it was minor. We spent a few days collating it, binding it, and mailing it out to an extensive distrib-ution list, all double-enveloped because of its Secret classification. This took some ingenuity because we didn't have enough envelopes and had to improvise using whatever large sheets of paper we could fold up to simulate envelopes. This worked, the only complaint being when the commandant of the Parachute School in Fort Benning, Colonel Jablonsky, an ex-All-American in football, visited us and noted that the double envelope scheme we used was not according to Hoyle. I looked at Colonel Norton and he looked back at me with a slight shrug as we accepted the criticism.

We now had in the enlisted group myself, Lange, Pritikin, Rohr, Wilhelm, Gilbertson, DeTomasso, Bulleit, Hidalgo, and some newer additions—Meyer, Law, Starr and Swope. Hidalgo had been reduced in rank to Corporal, which was not a punitive or disciplinary action but reflected his contributions to the group. We were, in truth, a very well organized and competent section, seasoned, with a strong nucle-us of men who had been through multiple campaigns.

Bulleit was somewhat of a complainer. He was one of those who volunteered for parachute duty as a way out of a dead-end situation in which he had been reduced from Staff Sergeant to Private. He came to us before Holland and we really used him because he was an excel-lent typist. As a new man he had been given duty at night, since we gave day duty preference to the guys who had been with us longest. He resented this and complained endlessly about the injustice of it all.

But he held his end up very well. Outside of the complaining, Don, a rather plain looking man, was quiet and kept very much to himself.

Years after the war I met him again and we talked and had a few meals together. He told me of his one great adventure while in the Army—one I hadn't heard about earlier because I was in England while it happened. The story also relates to Chester Dorant who was its hero. The Division had left Holland for its new base in Sissonne, France, where the post-Holland re-fitting took place. Convoys of trucks brought the weary troopers over those torn and bumpy roads, winding their way through Holland, Belgium and a considerable part of France.

The G-3 Section was loaded on a couple of trucks with its baggage, equipment and men. In the front of one truck with the driver was Dorant, in the rear were Bulleit and some of the other men. The convoy stopped for a short while in a French town and there was some jumping out to get a few beers from a brasserie and some jollying around with some girls. The convoy got going again and, as Bulleit related it, "Suddenly we noticed we had turned into a side street and the rest of the convoy kept going and we were finally alone in the town. Then the truck turned around and we headed back to the bar where we were greeted wildly by the girls we had left a short while earlier." The truck was parked out of sight in the rear and the five or six guys entered the bar, got gloriously drunk, and spent the night with the aforementioned girls. They were on the road early the following morning and arrived in Sissonne, late but hardly missed. It was, Don said, "the greatest thing that happened to me in my life, like something out of the movies!" It was Dorant's sole decision and he told the others that he would take full responsibility. As I have written earlier, Chester was well liked and this episode illustrates why.

We were fortunate to be serving under Colonel Norton, who was generally accepted to be the star of Headquarters, short of General Gavin. I have written about him earlier. One of the things about him was that he didn't issue orders to or dictate the usage or assignments of the enlisted men; he left that up to his subordinates. On the other hand, he was aware of how the section was run. Major Gerard and Captain Marston had been with us since Day One and were fixtures in G-3. Many officers had come and gone, some stopping with us for a month or two, some longer. Captain Graham had been with us since Normandy. Major Lekson came to us about this time from the 504th, as did Major Lee from the 307th Engineers. Captain Bridgewater was from the 508th and he acted as Liaison Officer to Corps Headquarters. Later, Lieutenants Smith and Toohey, as well as Major Novak, were with us for varying amounts of time. They were a good group.

I organized our men into groups with various functions, set up schedules for early and late duty, and established a working routine. While this was going on with us and other groups within Headquarters, the line outfits were receiving replacements, re-organizing, re-fitting and getting back into operational trim. This went on for a few weeks. Some men received passes, most of them opting to go to Paris; some few, who could make the arrangements, went to England. An interesting routine was set up. Someone or a group leaving for Paris on a pass would be assigned a jeep and an additional 5-gallon can of gasoline on the QT. This was the most precious black market commodity. In Paris this would be sold for a franc equivalent of $200, which was enough to bankroll a wild weekend.

My trip to Paris came in an interesting way. We had assigned to us a liaison officer from the Air Force, Major Thornton, and he had a 6-seater, single engine plane together with a crew chief, Sgt. Palmer. It was used to fly back and forth between headquarters and also from time to time by Gavin and other members of the staff. At this point we had a civilian specialist from the War Department, once again studying radar pathfinding, and he was to return to Washington after his study was concluded. He was returning by way of Paris and Norton suggested I take a quick one-nighter in Paris by joining Thornton and Palmer, who were transporting this specialist.

It didn't take me long to get ready and off we went, flying most unusually (at least for me). The plane flew at an altitude of a few hundred feet and followed the highways all the way in. We flew into LeBourget Field, which in my memory has always been connected with the 1927 flight of Lindbergh. There, we were met by a car from the US Embassy and driven into Paris, arriving as night was drawing near. There was no room for Palmer and me at the Embassy but the chauffeur drove us to a small nearby hotel where we checked in and had a meal and then were off to see the town. We wound up at the Moulin Rouge (where else?) which had been turned into a kind of Red Cross facility with tables covering most of the floor, leaving a small area for dancing, and a weary band up on the stage. Beer and wine flowed freely. Palmer and I were just getting settled when the nightly fight broke out and the place became a mad jumble of blows, curses, furniture being pushed around and broken and, finally, whistles as the MPs descended on the place in force. What I remember most is that the band kept bravely playing on—this probably happened all the time.

My suggestion was "Let's get out of here!" which we did as soon as we could. We found our way back through the darkened streets and awoke early the next day to spend the morning hours seeing what we could of the city. It was untouched by the ravages of war but very much down at the heels. I remember hardly anything of my first look at the City of Light. At noon we were back at the Embassy, ready for the return trip to Sissonne.

The break we had at the end of November and the first part of December didn't last long. Fortunately it lasted long enough for the Division to be brought back to strength, as was the 101st Division which was stationed some 40 miles away to the south and, together with us, constituted the entire reserve of the European Theater. All the other formations were committed to the line, which now stretched from Holland to Switzerland.

It was Sunday afternoon, which meant slack time, and I was attending a movie on the post, "Saratoga Trunk," with Ingrid Bergman and, I think, Clark Gable and a dwarf. I remember continually falling asleep during the movie, waking with a start, and then corking off again. When it was over, I sauntered back to the headquarters building to see if anything was going on, and immediately noticed nervous activity—something was in the air. That something, of course, was the German breakthrough in the Ardennes, and the subsequent assignments of we and our sister division to get up there as soon as possible.

We were to proceed immediately to the battle area, the 82d in the lead, to be followed by the 101st. Everybody had to be alerted, rations, ammunition and the like issued, and ready to be on the go the following day. This was an enormous task. We had to draw up the route to the battle area, decide on the order of march, mate the troops to be carried with the motor carriers available, establish time schedules, checkpoints, and draw up and publish the movement orders. The Colonel initiated the plans, turned it over to subordinates to refine, and then to us to execute. Needless to say, there were many re-dos and revisions. We toiled all night. I was without the services of Lange who had somehow disappeared, but showed up about 4 in the morning, disheveled, with a black eye and an anxious look.

Our skills had been honed in our previous engagements. What would have taken days we now did in a night. We worked right through to morning and the first troops were scheduled to leave that day. Norton had left when things seemed to be squared away and he joined Gavin and Colonel Ireland (G-1) up in the battle area. I was approached by Colonel Winton (G-2) and told I was to join him and Spotswood for a jeep dash up to the front. By this time, our work had been done, with the orders published and distributed. I ran back to my bunk, threw stuff together (remembering it was December), including the usual supply of cigarettes, and stowed it all in the back of the jeep together with that belonging to Winton, Spotswood and the driver, and off we went. We had been up all night.

19

WINTER IN THE ARDENNES

We were soon on the road, rattling our way in the jeep, Winton and the driver up front and Jim Spotswood and me in the rear. It was an overcast day in mid-December; winter hadn't settled in as yet. The French roads had taken quite a beating in spots, not being designed to carry the traffic of ponderous tanks and their metal treads. A smooth or rough ride depended on the skill of the driver who, at times, had to navigate through some very broken and pitted spots.

Some towns we hurried through were in good shape, others that had seen a battle or the bombing of a crossroads were semi-destroyed. France, we noted, would have a massive rebuilding job after the war. On occasion we would pass pockmarked fields where bombs meant for the road net or railway in a nearby town had landed harmlessly. So much, we thought, for precision bombing.

We headed for Houffalize, which was the central one of a string of three towns on a north-south highway between Luxembourg in the south and Liege (Belgium) in the north. The other crossroads towns were Bastogne to the south and Werbomont to the north. The east-west roads running through the three towns all led into Germany some 30 to 40 miles to the east where the breakthrough by the enemy had taken place along a wide front.

As we approached Houffalize in the early afternoon we could sense something was wrong. Somehow one got used to a certain order of things in rear areas—the outward appearance of groups of men and vehicles, their direction and demeanor, etc. Among other things, it became apparent that we had our side of the road to ourselves, the other side being increasingly crowded with a mixed jumble of vehicles, ordnance and men going in the other direction. We passed groups of apparently aimless soldiers sitting on the side of the road. Then it dawned on us. They were retreating! It was hard to believe. Regardless of the problem at the front, which we thought to be many miles away, we were passing through a perfectly peaceful area. The appearance of the troops and their air of defeat was incongruous given the surroundings and was odd to us. Every now and then Colonel Winton would have to stand up in the front of the jeep and at the top his voice order the road in front of us to be cleared so that we could proceed. We were a band of four, soon to be followed by the combined strength of the two Airborne Divisions. Everybody else was going in the other direction. It was strange.

The same disorder prevailed in Houffalize when Winton went into a frazzled and disorganized VIII Corps Headquarters for further instructions. It had developed that the immediate danger and aim of the enemy in what was soon to be called the Battle of the Bulge was perceived to be the city of Liege to the north, which contained huge dumps of supplies including gasoline. Heavy German armored penetrations had taken place, seemingly headed in that direction. So the decision had been taken to send the 82d, the first on the road, to Werbomont on the road to Liege, and the 101st, following us by a day, to Bastogne.

To the north we went on a journey, some of which is as clear today as when we did it. As we left Houffalize we still encountered fleeing troops. But soon we were on a deserted road, going at the highest speed that could be coaxed out of the jeep. We were alone on the road and Winton advised us to have our weapons loaded and at the ready in case we ran into Germans. In the shadows of the afternoon, as we grew colder, we hurried on, realizing that we were in some version of no-man's land, all-senses attuned to what might appear around the next bend. On one occasion we passed a large group of burning vehicles across a field. There was no way of knowing in the gathering twilight whether they were ours or theirs and how they came to be on fire. Obviously there had been a recent battle. We just kept speeding on, one lonely jeep. As daylight was waning and the chill settling in, we, with a collective sigh of relief, reached the town of Werbomont, which was little more than a crossroads. There, inside a deserted hotel/bar were Norton and Ireland (the G-1) and our presence just about doubled the 82d's numbers in Belgium. There were also a few stragglers from other outfits who had decided to stay put and not flee.

In the darkness, the formations of the 82d began to arrive. The first directive was to assign areas of the battlefield to the units as they arrived, cold and stiff from their day-long confinement in the back of trucks. We had been assigned a unit of quartermaster vehicles from Army, which consisted of a fleet of huge trucks manned by black troops, that stayed with us through the whole battle and joined us on other occasions for the remainder of the war. They did the bulk of the hauling of men and supplies, working alongside our normal complement of vehicles.

Winton had picked up some maps in Houffalize and I put together a map covering the area, which was used to direct the various formations as they arrived. We soon became a bustling headquarters with all the functions of the Division operating out of this one room, which was part of a cafe lit by candle and lantern. Toward morning, not having slept the night before, I crawled under a table with conversation, shuffling boots and people swirling around, and fell fast asleep.

The Bulge was the first battle in which we did not arrive at the battlefield in piecemeal fashion. All the 82d's infantry regiments, four in all, arrived at the battlefield in order, together with their ancillary formations, so the staff was able to position them and plan the battle as "normal" units did. Later in the battle we were joined by the 517th Parachute Regiment and the 551st Parachute Battalion, which had entered France from the Mediterranean. That gave us a total of 16 infantry battalions, far exceeding our normal complement. In addition, we were assigned tanks, tank destroyers and large caliber artillery from higher headquarters, thus making up for our shortcomings in these areas and beefing us up to a splendid fighting machine.

In the first hours of the battle, before we arrived, American units on the northern shoulder of the Bulge had held their ground, forcing delay on the German 6th Panzer Army and forcing a shift in the German emphasis toward the south. There, deep penetrations were made by the 5th Panzer Army against our line, which was held in that area only by one green and one battered and refitting Division.

Penetrations in the center had bypassed the town of St. Vith, which was held steadfastly by our 7th Armored Division. Our assignment was to establish contact with our forces on the northern shoulder of the Bulge, sealing off any attempts by the Germans to advance in that direction, and also to reach out and make contact with the 7th Armored.

The first into-the-breach days of fighting put us face to face with both the 1st and 9th SS Panzer Divisions. We advanced to the lines which were our objectives and held firm, blunting the force of the 6th Panzer Army, which had been slowed down earlier in their attacks on the northern shoulder. Fierce engagements were fought with Task Force Peiper, which had been the spearhead unit of 1st SS Panzer and which had committed the massacre of American prisoners at Malmedy. But now they were rendered useless by the mauling they took from us.

I remember one morning, early in the battle, when General Gavin stopped by to study the Operations map on his way to make his rounds of the units. The 101st at the time was surrounded at Bastogne and I had drawn a complete circle around the town indicating their beleaguered state. He looked at it for a moment or two and then muttered to no one in particular, "Those barroom brawlers of the One-oh-One have them exactly where they want them." I thought that was kind of neat.

In a matter of days the weather turned cold, we were suddenly in winter, and were blanketed with snow. In addition, for the first week, our Air Force was unable to contribute because of the overcast and cloudy weather. Conditions for the infantryman became intolerable. Later on there was an issue of shoe paks, warm socks and sweaters, but men never got used to living 24 hours on and in the frozen ground in snowy conditions. It was close to unbearable duty. Contrary to our usual practice of functioning outdoors, we established our movable headquarters in a series of farmhouses, mainly using the kitchens, which were the largest rooms in the houses and where there was always a stove. We carried additional blankets with which to black out the windows.

The XVIIIth Airborne Corps was given command of the sector we were in so we once again were joined with Ridgway. After we had pushed out, established contact with the 7th Armored so they could withdraw from St. Vith, and reached a favorable line of high ground from which to conduct further activities, orders came down from Field Marshal Montgomery (who had been given command of the northern section of the battle) to withdraw to a shorter line while preparations for an eventual attack were made. This withdrawal was made over the objections of both Ridgway and Gavin and was the first time we had ever withdrawn. Some time later we were given the order to re-take what we had given up, which we did with the inevitable loss of men.

In Holland, Montgomery, as Army Group commander, had bypassed his Army and Corps commands and gone directly to the Divisions for a view of what was happening. In a system that would not be tolerated in our Army he set up an operation called Phantom. Phantom placed a small group, usually led by a major, with a powerful radio that was in contact with Monty's HQ, at each Division in the command. Their job was to stay aware of activities within the divisional areas and report directly (bypassing the intermediate commands) back to their central installation, which gave the information to Montgomery.

Sure enough, after a few days of battle in the Ardennes, a jeep pulled up and this English major strode in, announcing that he was Montgomery's eyes and ears and that he had carte blanche to any and all information. He came at a time when things were a little hectic and, with a few winks being exchanged between our Provost Marshal, Major McCallum and others, the English Major was arrested under suspicion of being a spy. The joke lasted long enough for everyone to have a good laugh, and the good major was released with much puffing and sputtering.

After the Germans were stopped in the Ardennes, many sharp battles were fought. At one point we were relieved and rested up for a few days and were then recommitted in the attack through the Siegfried Line into Germany. We were once again relieved, rested and then sent into a battle near the Roer Dams, which became impossible when the enemy purposely broke the dams and flooded the surrounding area. All in all, we spent two months in battle, accounted ourselves with distinction and returned to France in early February.

We moved our headquarters many times during the battle.

Although we changed around a little bit, usually I had Wilhelm, Lange, and Pritikin with me in the advance CP. We were typically located where the local network of roads permitted contact with all the major units of the command. This usually meant about 1,500 yards behind the front line, far from rifle and machine gun fire but well within artillery range of the Germans. The fire was heaviest during the day but even the long hours of the night were sprinkled with sporadic activity, some seemingly close to us but none, fortunately, finding us precisely.

We adapted to the routine and could break down our equipment in a few minutes and re-establish it in a new location just as quickly. We kept our materials at the ready in those ammunition boxes, including supplies. The few items of furniture (folding tables and chairs), along with the map board, typewriters, etc. came along and we could actually move the necessary items for the function of G-3 in two jeep trailers—one if all that was available to us was one jeep.

In one of these moves, we were in a small convoy of jeeps when we stopped in an open area of a small town in eastern Belgium. In this part of the country the towns had German rather than French names because they were in part of a zone that had been ceded to Belgium after World War I to act as a buffer between the two countries. It was about midday and Spotswood and I sat on a curb at the side of the road and opened up some K-rations for lunch. There had obviously been a battle and some intensive activity in this town only a short while earlier.

There were destroyed German vehicles strewn about, some of them still smoldering, and there was the odor of explosives in the air. Also numerous dead bodies, all enemy. As we began to eat, we began to check out the scene and idly discuss the carnage before us, speculating which dead body went with what shattered halftrack, etc. This becomes grisly because there were also some dismembered bodies among the dead and we began, in a matter of fact way, to try and match up the various pieces. There was one particular leg, encased in a trouser leg and boot, which we couldn't figure out.

All this while we were eating! Suddenly the complete idiocy of the wreckage, the dead bodies, the body parts and eating K-rations while observing it all, struck me, and I started to giggle and then laugh almost uncontrollably, as close to hysteria as I ever came. We both stopped eating after a few bites and were ready to move on.

There was one stage of the battle when we were positioned in line with the 1st Infantry Division (Big Red One) and given objectives side by side, which had to be taken through deep snow. Major Lekson was given the assignment of going over to their headquarters, establish contact with them and establish the protocol by which we would operate side by side. Lekson was a big, handsome guy and he came over to me and said, "Why don't you come along with me and see how the other half lives?" And further, "But let's look sharp and not wear our helmets." This non-helmet thing was going to be an obvious dig at the location of their headquarters, which was some miles behind the front line.

So I cleaned up as best I could, brushed off my boots, and dug out my overseas cap from the recesses of my bag and off we went into the cold, dark evening. We made our point, striding into their CP as if we were on parade, oblivious to the stares being thrown our way. But, compared to the way we operated, they were the Ritz and we a $2 motel. They had all their equipment mounted in special enclosed trailers (with electricity) that didn't have to be dismantled for each change of locale. They seemed to have twice the staff we had. But we had made our impressive entrance and enjoyed doing it. Before leaving I helped myself to a couple of handfuls of grease pencils (sometimes we were down to tiny stubs) and some other goodies which I stuffed into my pockets, and then back to our plain pipe rack headquarters.

Like most of the others, I had latched on to some things that I thought indispensable, while discarding others. The first thing everybody dumped was the gas mask, which was redistributed each time we were re-fitted but were only good as an extra place to carry cigarettes. We had all been issued carbines as our basic weapon, which fired the standard .30-caliber bullet but with much less muzzle velocity and accuracy than the M-1 rifle. So at first opportunity I had commandeered an M-1, as did most infantrymen in our rifle companies. The parachute riflemen had been issued folding stock versions of the carbine, which folded into a weapon not much larger than an automatic pistol. Great for lack of bulk in a parachute jump but less than that as an infantry weapon.

I got hold of a musette bag, which I made my own. This bag, about 4x10x15 inches, made out of flexible twill material, was indispensable. Into this I could put everything I needed, including a couple of days rations. Other items were shaving stuff, toilet paper, my ever-present length of rope, underwear, socks, writing materials, mess kit and utensils, cigarettes, grease pencils, flints for the Zippo lighter I carried in my pocket, and other goodies. The lighter was a must because of the lack of matches and it performed the function of lighting lanterns and fires in stoves and fireplaces.

Equally important to us was to keep at least one 5-gallon can of water on hand for our group, and also a 5-gallon can of gasoline. The latter was for cooking (the biscuit tin method), for the temperamental Coleman lanterns and for the Zippo lighters. The lighters were equipped with their distinctive cage around the wick, which permitted them to be used in all kinds of weather. The interior works slid out of the outer sheath and could be dipped as a whole into the can of gasoline for re-fueling, using a straightened out paper clip as a hook.

About personal appearance: As a matter of pride, we tried to look as good as we could, which meant shaving every day if possible. This wasn't always doable, because it meant heating up water—not available sometimes, but we did the best we could. In this respect we were unconsciously following the lead of General Gavin, who always had an air of elegance about him, even while he was prowling the front line carrying his rifle in his clenched hand, slightly bent over as he walked. So, we all fell in line, which, oddly, gave us a certain feeling of accomplishment—we could overcome the environment. Even so, toward the end of the battle, I started to grow a moustache, trimming it as best I could to avoid looking silly. It was coming along nicely when Colonel Norton gave me a quizzical look and asked, "Do you really think you look good in that thing?" Enough said, and with a sigh it came off the next day. (So much for courage under fire.)

For some time, up to and including the Belgian campaign, there had been a limited rotation of men from units that had been in battle for extended periods. And so it was that one man per month, for a number of months, had been sent on this rotation back to the States from Division Headquarters Company. I have referred earlier, in describing the days preceding D-Day in France, the peculiar relationship between Headquarters and Headquarters Company, wherein administratively (which would include selecting someone for rotation) this decision would be made by HQ Co.

This kind of annoyed us because we didn't feel we were being considered. So, after some discussions among us, Master Sergeants Soady (G-1), Morton (G-4) and Spotswood and I decided to approach the Headquarters commandant, Major Johnson, about the seeming unfairness. One afternoon in the town of Rott, we requested and received an "audience" with Johnson. He listened and from that point on, Headquarters was included in the pool from which the "rotatee" was selected. At least one guy was sent from the Adjutant General's office. We had made our point.

Much has been written about that winter. It was truly cold and miserable. The snow came just before Christmas and was there throughout the entire battle. If it melted at all, it immediately froze and became worse. At times, tanks and other tracked vehicles became useless because they slid off the road or became menaces as they blocked the narrow way. Digging a hole by the infantryman became a labor of frustrating exhaustion. Fingers and feet literally froze. Frostbite was common, as was a new malady, trench foot, caused by a combination of cold and moisture in the confines of a dirty sock and boot. The Army came up with a new item—shoe pacs, which were a combination of a heavy waterproof overshoe with a removable felt liner. It helped somewhat. On one of our moves, I was seated in the rear of the jeep all bundled up. It was a short trip of only about 20 minutes but I felt my right cheek becoming numb from the cold. I had a slight case of frostbite, which really hurt and tingled as it eventually thawed out. But I was truly fortunate compared to those men who had to function in that cold, out in the open, under fire, with nothing to look forward to but tomorrow being the same.

Major Lee of our section came up with a brilliant idea (or at least took credit for it). He was a West Pointer and the son of Lt. General Lee who was in command of the Services of Supply for the entire European Theater, a big job. Our Lee was commissioned in the Engineer Corps and gave the outward impression of being anything but a fighting man; he was roundish, shuffled around and seemed diffident about everything. The idea he came up with stemmed from the difficulties we were having moving traffic in and out of the area because of the narrow roads, the heavy comings and goings and the aforementioned problems of the tracked vehicles which often resulted in severe holdups. Lee laid a piece of overlay paper over the map and traced out a system whereby all roads became one way and all intersections would be monitored by an MP whose job would be to allocate time through the intersection to alternating directions. It worked!

Lee also was involved in an act of derring-do straight out of Mission Impossible. He volunteered for an assignment to blow up a small bridge in the German road net on the other side of the line. Together with a small crew, he crept up to the bridge in the dark of night, attached the explosive charges and took cover in the underbrush. He waited until there were enemy vehicles on the bridge and then he blew it up. Lee was cited for the Distinguished Service Cross for the exploit.

We constantly scrounged for supplies and rations. Whenever I could I hoarded additional items for the group and had everybody on the look-out for opportunities to squirrel things away. The Army came up with some other ideas for feeding beyond C's and K's, namely 5-in-ones and, later, 10-in-ones. In those cases the ration container included food for one day for 5 (or 10) men, and included goodies such as canned fruit and bacon. We managed not to go hungry and became adept at preparing food using the British biscuit-tin method that we learned in Holland. Packages from home, which we received intermittently with our mail, were welcome additions to our scruffy fare.

The Army helped out on occasions. A major effort was made on Christmas Day for everybody to have a hot turkey dinner and it was welcomed by all (even though some had to wait a day to get theirs). The Christmas dinner coincided with the lifting of the weather over the battlefield and the welcome appearance of our Air Force, which was wildly cheered by all.

It was a long battle. Despite all we did to keep reasonably clean and dry, sleeping in filthy cellars with no change of clothes got to us in the form of various itching diseases. Many of us scratched constantly. On one occasion I was driving with Norton in a jeep, going I forget where, when we passed a series of long, low tents with welcome smoke curling from their smokestacks. Norton ordered the jeep to stop and we discovered that this was a portable bath outfit similar to the one I had found in Normandy. Without hesitation, Norton hopped out, told Cooke (the driver) and me to follow, and we went in for a glorious 3-minute bath. You removed your clothes, took your insignia off the uniform, disposed of your clothes, except shoes, and filed into a room-sized area with a series of troughs, each under a perforated pipe. Once in a trough with a group of about eight men, the water was turned on and poured out through the perforations in the pipes. One minute was for getting wet, one minute was for applying soap and the third minute was for rinsing off. The water was blessedly hot and we emerged feeling like newborn babes. Armed only with our shoes and insignia, we were then led through another area where underwear and a completely new uniform were issued. We were aglow!

For a number of reasons, I felt we were at our best in this battle. We went in as a whole unit, were reinforced with heavy artillery, tanks and transport, and were able to present a unified face on the battlefield. We had an experienced command and a strong cadre of leaders on all levels. Under the constraints and necessities of the battle, however, we took severe losses. By the end of it, as we headed back to France and Sissonne, most of the infantry companies had very few of the original men who had left Fort Bragg almost two years earlier. There was consequently upward mobility among the survivors: lieutenants became majors, privates became platoon sergeants, and the like.

Our headquarters (not only G-3) had become very professional. We had some attrition but nothing even remotely comparing to the line outfits. We had basically discarded all the fluff and had learned to thrive on a bare minimum in very adverse circumstances. We, officers and men alike, had become good at what we did. Pritikin had given me the sobriquet "The Whip," which Hidalgo pronounced "Weep," and Lucky Meyer, a new addition, translated into German as "Der Vip." It seemed to be all in good fun.

One of life's little embarrassments came somewhere in the middle of the battle. The after-battle report for Holland which I had shepherded through production in England had been distributed to all and sundry. While in Belgium there arrived, addressed to General Gavin, a letter from Supreme Commander Eisenhower, congratulating him on the fine publication. This, of course, was fairly routine, and most units who included Ike on their distribution list probably received a similar letter. Now Gavin did not have a personal staff so he turned it over to Weinecke, our Chief of Staff, who also did not have a working staff, so he turned it over to Colonel Norton, who, after it was shown around, entrusted it to me for safekeeping. It was a trophy of sorts, the type that grows more important with time. After it was perused by all, I had it placed in one of our carry-all ammunition boxes, assuming all would be in order. Imagine my dismay when several days later it was discovered to be missing!

Searches through all of our limited section baggage didn't turn it up. After discussing it with our men, I felt convinced none of us knew what had happened. And, really, there was no place to hide it, so I felt that the guilty one, if anybody, was outside of the ranks of our enlisted group. I had the unpleasant task of reporting its loss to Colonel Weinecke and accepting responsibility, since it had been entrusted to me. He accepted my explanation.

Which brings me to the officer-enlisted man relationship within our group. As I have written earlier, we were fortunate in being led by outstanding men, from Ridgway and Gavin on down. Weinecke and Norton were fine men and understood the proper relationship, which was, basically, that officers had their job and enlisted men theirs and both had to respect the relationship. Problems arose when officers (such as Colonel Rusk) did not show that respect but took advantage of their rank.

At one point in the early stage of the Bulge, we were being moved to another area of the battle and were relieved by an outfit newly arrived from the States, the 75th Infantry Division. We felt for them. They arrived and climbed down nervously from the backs of the trucks that brought them, looking squeaky clean in their heavy over-coats, clean helmets, gloves, shoes, rifles, etc., and they must have looked at some of us who were dirty and bedraggled, oddly uni-formed, unshaven, slouching, and wondered where we came from and what they were getting into. The Army had an expression for that feel-ing—"Is this trip necessary?" Anyway, as with most new outfits, the 75th took their initial setbacks, consolidated, and then gave a good account of themselves.

At our final relief in February 1945, the understrength Division was loaded back onto the same trucks that had brought us to Belgium. We threw our stuff into one of the HQ 2-1/2-ton trucks and got into our jeeps and reversed our way to Sissonne over the same pitted roads we had traveled two months earlier. In the interim, the last offensive gasp of the Germans had been defeated, and victory was now really in sight, although there was more fighting before it would happen.

For our part, we had functioned beautifully as a headquarters group, starting with Norton, down through all the section. Our enlisted men did well and I was pleased with myself and all the others. Later, I received the Bronze Star for this campaign and even later I was awarded the Belgian Croix de Guerre, one of fourteen awarded to the Division.

20

REFITTING ONCE MORE

Tired relief. Those words described the feeling after the rigors of the campaign in the Ardennes. The Division, though victorious and firm in its belief in its invincibility, was tired and its ranks were sadly thinned.

We loaded in the jeeps and trucks, thankful that we had individually made it (although so many didn't), but weary in the wake of this, our fifth major campaign. The toll had been significant. Most of the line outfits were seriously understrength and, though still battle-worthy, had few of their original men being counted in the company morning reports.

One of the increasingly obvious facts about all of this is that most of the time Headquarters personnel, no matter how close to the battle, lived to talk about it and are present for another day. So it was with me, Lange, Spotswood and the rest. We had seen war and horror but did not have to face it, non-ending, with only the muzzle of a rifle between you and one of the enemy who is as dedicated to killing you as you are to him.

But the defeat of the Germans in the recent battle had been so crushing that it was obvious that they were beaten and that it was only a matter of time before the end. Unfortunately, there was no question that despite this, there would be serious fighting ahead as the Germans would rally in defense of their homeland once the battle was carried there. In this mood we returned to our base in Sissonne, got clean uniforms, mail from home, hot meals, showers and, for many, passes to Paris and England.

By now, my son was more that a year old, was talking and, from all reports, was growing into a vigorous, healthy young lad. It was hard for that to sink in. Alice kept me up to date on all the news with a never-ending stream of letters.

We were now located in a tent city rather than the concrete barracks we had inhabited during our earlier stay. The tent area was located a few hundred feet from the headquarters building and mess hall so, distance-wise, was more convenient than earlier. As I recall, there were about 50 tents for our headquarters and associated groups, most tents having six inhabitants. The first row of tents, however, included a series of pairs of 6 x 9 wall tents, assembled end to end, making an elongated 6 x 18-foot tent. These tents were assigned to the ranking NCO's, and Spotswood and I, who shared one, were given the ranking spot of the first tent in the first row. This became crucial to an event I will describe later on.

It was time for us to regroup. We had two rooms in the headquarters, each being about 15 x 30 feet. One was established as the main room, with Colonel Norton and most of his officers in one end and me and whoever was manning the phone and journal in the other. In the second room, a couple of the junior officers and the rest of the men were established along with all the files, supplies and reproducing equipment, etc.

A new Table of Organization had come out for an Airborne Division, and our enlisted complement was expanded far beyond what it was back in the Ft. Bragg days. We now had two Staff Sergeants allocated. One obvious choice was Willis Lange, who had put in the most quality time over the longest period and had been given a promotion when I was elevated to Master Sergeant. The other promotion should have been given to Pritikin, Rohr or Wilhelm, but went instead to Louis Edison, who had been transferred from the 505th where he'd held the rank of T/4 (three stripes). Why he came to us at this time never was made clear but I assume he had run into some difficulties or a dead-end in the 505th and the Colonel brought him on board with us. At the time, Pritikin was a buck Sergeant and the other two were T/4's. Rohr was then made Sergeant, which had only symbolic meaning because the change made no difference in pay or rank. If Pritikin or Wilhelm were put out by these developments, they said nothing about it, and Lange had been overjoyed at his promotion. The one who didn't take it well was Rohr who added this to his already long list of grumbles. Edison turned out to be fine and did his best to fit into the group.

One of our first jobs was assembling and putting out the after-action report for the Battle of the Bulge. During a lull in the battle, General Gavin had written a report covering the first two weeks of the battle, which he delivered in person to various groups. It was truly a masterful piece and became the cornerstone for the entire report. Lucky Meyer, an addition just before the battle, was an accomplished artist and he created the cover for it, which featured a de-tracked German tank with its cannon barrel shattered.

The usual training cycle was inaugurated, starting with filling our replacements in the various platoons and companies. This was culminated by a Division Review which I viewed from a window on the second floor corridor, keeping solid my record of never having stood a formation like that after my first week in the Army, when we new recruits were stand-on-the-sideline witnesses of a review.

We also had a mass practice parachute jump which was marred by fatalities when a plane stalled after its men had jumped and fell to the ground through the descending men, clipping some of the chutes and causing a few deaths. Miraculously, though, one trooper rode on the tail of the plane all the way to its landing and survived! There was a belated ceremony pinning jump wings on those who had taken the training when I did. There is a picture of it I have in which Gavin is addressing us and everybody is spiffed up to the nines.

And the War Room. It was once again constituted and bigot cards were distributed. This time the planning was concentrated on the "what if" of a sudden German collapse and our being called upon to drop on Berlin to take control. This was called Operation Eclipse, and existed over time in many variations. We were, indeed, kept busy.

Diversionary events included a series of affairs wherein groups of men were trucked into town for an evening party, which featured lots of food and included townspeople and one of our two bands playing dance music. Our turn came. I had volunteered to be in the last truck returning to our camp, which would include a small clean-up crew and the dishes which had been used for the party. The party featured a near fight between Rohr and Edison, which I had to break up by getting between them.

Outside of the near fight, most everybody enjoyed themselves. A few liaisons were made but it was obvious the main attraction the party had for the townies were the tables groaning with food, fruit and drink. Their eyes popped, not having seen anything like that in years. Some wine was served and there was a festive air. Then the clean-up detail, which I was to check on, loaded all the dishes and leftovers, including some wine, into the back of a 2-1/2-ton truck for the trip back to camp.

All was in order and everyone in a good mood as we proceeded back to Sissonne. A group of guys in the back of the truck, somewhat high on the wine, were having a great time singing and laughing, and then they decided to punctuate their songs by scaling dishes, one by one, from the truck. One of the detail in the back, alarmed at the depletion of the dishes, now being scattered over some miles of French landscape, tried unsuccessfully to stop it, and then frantically signaled up to the front of the truck where I was that something was amiss. The truck finally stopped. Sgt. Rinehart, who was in charge of the dishes, pulled the laughing offenders out of the truck and a battle royal ensued in the dark, on this lonely road in the middle of France. Outside the loss of the dishes, it was a hilarious affair with bodies and dishes flying all over the terrain. When it calmed down with an abused Rinehart the obvious victor, the summary punishment we handed down was that the offenders were thrown off the truck for the remainder of the trip and had to make the rest of their way back to camp on their own. The story was told and retold over the ensuing days with never-ending embellishment.

But then another adventure unfolded, this time involving Spotswood and me and a glamorous war correspondent. Martha Gellhorn was the correspondent, a woman probably in her thirties who, at the time, was married to Ernest Hemingway, the most famous American writer of the day and also a reporter on the war. Martha was quite well known, considered by some to be the best female correspondent. She made her way around the war zones on her own, in a jeep, not taking advantage of the Army's offer to furnish her with a driver (who would also be her bodyguard). She had showed up in

Holland and stayed with us for some weeks while she prepared a number of articles about the Division which appeared principally in *Colliers* magazine, a mass circulation periodical of the day. Rumor had it that she spent a lot of time with General Gavin.

On one particularly slow Sunday while we were in Sissonne, she came into our mess hall to "mix with the troops" at dinner, which, on Sunday, was served in the late afternoon, there being only two meals served on Sundays. We all noticed her, paying not too much attention. After eating I went out the back to wash off my mess kit in the usual set up of three large garbage cans filled with hot water; the first was soapy, in which you cleaned off the remaining food from your plate with a brush, the second and third cans having clean water in which you plunged your kit in succession to clean off the soap. As one can imagine, after a hundred or so men do this without the water being changed, sanitation is out the window. But we were all young and healthy, so we survived.

And there, standing beyond the last can was Spotswood, engaged in animated conversation with Gellhorn. Now, Jim had been a newspaper writer in Meriden, Mississippi, was a speaker with great charm and courtliness, and he had her fully engaged with his talk. Taking advantage of my buddy-buddy relationship with Jimmy, I sidled over to the two of them and joined Jimmy's urging when he advised Martha that he had a bottle of Scotch in our tent (news to me) and would she join us for a drink. And this is where the position of our tent in the first row and rank came into play—it was not too far away and we wouldn't have to parade through a tent street in order to get there. So she agreed to join us and we stepped the few paces to our tent, staying in my end of the tent while Jimmy rummaged through his belongings and emerged with his bottle of Johnny Walker whisky.

The afternoon was growing dark and we lit a flickering lantern and sat, two of us on my cot and the other on my barracks bag, and began to attack the booze. Our interest was the same, although we didn't discuss it. We wanted to hear about her adventures, particularly in the Spanish Civil War, where she had met Hemingway and which seemed very romantic to us. We also had many questions about her husband and her methods of operation. She, in turn, was mining us for material, which she may or may not have seen fit to use in her writings. It was a heady time for Jimmy and me and we were enjoying every moment as we passed our dirty canteen cups around, alternately with whisky and then water from the five-gallon can we kept in the tent.

After about an hour of this (and it can not be emphasized how engaging this was to Jimmy and me), as we grew steadily drunk, including Gellhorn, she suddenly cried out in exasperation, after one more reference to her husband, "Enough of Hemingway. Fuck Ernest Hemingway!" Well, you could have knocked us over with a feather but we looked at each other, laughed and raised the cup and bottle, and in chorus, repeated her exclamation

Soon we were singing songs of the day, for example, "There are blue birds over the white cliffs of Dover . . ." and then ending with, "F--- Ernest Hemingway." We did this with any number of songs, finishing each chorus with "F--- Ernest Hemingway." We were then clutching each other, gasping for air as we tried to suppress our laughter (not wanting to make too much noise) and rolling off the canvas cot onto the dirt floor. It was sheer, booze-induced hilarity, which went on for some time until we realized the potentially compromising circumstance of two soldiers and the guest of the general carousing in the soldiers' tent.

Slowly we calmed down. The gales of laughter became chuckles and then sighs and we settled down contentedly. The Scotch was drying up, we had been in our tent for about two hours, it was dark out and we realized that somewhere an alarm was being raised for the missing Martha. Actually, she was the soberest of the three. We decided, among the fondest of farewells, that she would have to leave and return to her temporary digs, which were at the other end of the camp where the top brass was. We self-consciously pulled ourselves together, declaring we would see her home, etc. She would have none of this (probably for our protection), referred to her jeep, which was close by, and her ability to drive it the half-mile or so to where she would bed down.

We half staggered to the tent fly, opened it, and to our amazement, it seemed as if the whole encampment was outside listening to the events going on in our tent. After all, a female visitor in the area just didn't happen, and an English speaking one at that. With exaggerated

calm, we ignored the crowd and walked with her to her jeep, exchanged hugs and she was off.

The next morning, everybody was looking at us at breakfast and
we just looked at each other (Jimmy and I) and picked through our
meal. Obviously, the word was all over the camp and this would mean
at the officer's end as well. But nothing was ever said to us, although
we received many a searching look. Jimmy and I, by tacit agreement,
refrained from discussing the escapade with anybody and eventually it
blew over.

For us, it had been a great evening and it came just a couple of
days before once again there were the stirrings before a major move.
Our troops had advanced to the Rhine River, there was a major operation being planned in the north (again with Montgomery being reinforced with an American Army—the Ninth), the American First Army
had seized a bridge over the Rhine at Remagen, and Third Army was
closing to the Rhine on the south. There was a sizable length of the
Rhine around Cologne which was relatively quiet but needed some
bolstering. So we were earmarked for that area and, as March drew to
a close, we were on the road once again.

21

FINAL CAMPAIGN
AND VICTORY

Cologne was a major city on the Rhine, and apparently did not have as much military importance as some other areas. This possibly had to do with the terrain it fronted inside Germany, which was not tactically attractive as a roadway for an attacking force. The city had been severely damaged—flattened might be a better word—by a series of major air attacks over a considerable length of time. Its transportation system was gone and the availability of utilities severely limited. A jeep foray into the city showed huge chunks of reinforced concrete laying about, turned-over and destroyed trolley cars, and nothing but devastation. Cologne was mainly deserted.

Two major sites seemed to have escaped damage: the famous Gothic Cathedral, which was on the banks of the river near the railroad station, and a large Ford factory which was on the city's northern edge. The escape of the factory led to much cynical commentary.

Our troops were strung out along the length of river in the area, which included the city. Headquarters was established in a small villa in a northern suburb, which was mainly undamaged. My crew and I located ourselves in a three-story house which was deserted but undamaged, and most of the other men were nearby. The houses were without utilities or running water but we managed to get some heat going in the room, using space stoves to warm up water for bathing and shaving as we needed it. All in all, living was not too bad.

As mentioned, we were on a very quiet front and not there for any offensive reasons, but our troops along the Rhine were so used to action that some routine patrolling led, in one case, to one of the reg-

189

iments exploiting ground held by a patrol to place elements of a battalion on the far bank of the river. This happened while Patton was
probing for a crossing farther south and Montgomery, in the north,
was almost repeating the build-up that went into the Normandy landings for his crossing of the Rhine near Wesel. The Wesel operation was
to be spearheaded by the 6th British and 17th US Airborne Divisions,
organized with Ridgway, this time, in charge. The airborne landings
turned out to be a huge success.

Meanwhile, some consternation ensued in our area because of the
unauthorized crossing by the aforementioned troops, who were summarily ordered to come back to our side of the river. This they did,
though with much grumbling. So we were in an unusual front-line situation, facing the enemy across a swath of the wide river with both
sides being equally spread out. The Germans had defensive positions
that included machine gun emplacements along the river front.

On our side of the river were a series of warehouses with at least
one of them reportedly full of wine. These warehouses fronted the
river and were accessible through the network of city streets including
one that ran parallel with the river. If one drove along that street, the
warehouses would offer protection from fire ranging from the other
side, except when passing over a cross street which would place one
momentarily in sight of someone looking over from across the river.

Chasing the questionable prize of the wine (which I really didn't
like) I foolishly ran the gauntlet along with my driver, winding up at
the wine warehouse. There we filled a couple of five gallon cans with
the stuff and raced back, followed by the sound of some ineffective
machine gun fire from across the river. Stupid, but we did it. I did no
more than taste the wine but others received it gratefully.

One of the results of the wine hoard was that Hidalgo became
roaring drunk. As I have written earlier, he was perhaps the most universally liked within our group, with his easy smile and fractured
English. He was a chaser of women and in his inebriated state
announced that he was out to find a fraulein. There was a rule called
"non-fraternization," which basically prohibited any social contact
with German civilians. In his wild state we had to forcibly hold him
down and I was concerned that he might bust loose and get into a situation that would be difficult to bail him out of. Our mess was locat-

ed in the rear courtyard of a nearby house and, as we left our house for lunch, we locked Hidalgo in a third floor bathroom with admonitions for him to stay put.

Off I went to eat with the others and the meal was halfway down when a rustle and disturbance announced the arrival of Hidalgo, who had obviously pulled a Houdini in getting out of that locked room. He was whooping it up and hugging everyone and kept draping himself over me in an amiable state uttering his version of my name as "Weep, Weep!" With the aid of the others I was finally able to get him back to our building (he was quite strong) and found that he had left the third floor bathroom by a thin wire clothes line and lowered himself hand over hand to the other end of the line which was tethered to a pole which he then climbed down. It seemed impossible, but apparently he did it. We had to stay with him and forcibly restrain him until the wine wore off and he had sobered up. We then made sure to keep him away from the remainder of the wine.

It was about this time that Colonel Norton called me aside and asked me if I wanted to go to Officer's Candidate School! After all the disappointments and dashing of hopes earlier in the game, now, with the war tapering down, came the opportunity. I repressed my thoughts and told him I would let him know my answer quickly. I soon found out that, at the same time Norton was talking to me, Colonel Winton, the G-2, was making the same proposal to Jimmy Spotswood.

It posed a real dilemma. We all knew the war was winding down. The German defenses were in a shambles, and soon the Allied armies would be chasing all across Germany on a many-pronged front. Both of us on one hand were dying to go to OCS, but not at the expense of having to stay in the Army any longer than necessary, or being included in a force that would invade Japan after the end of hostilities in Europe. We talked it over and agreed our best course was to decline the offer. The worst part was that we had to decide quickly and did not have time to reflect or consult with our wives, which would have taken weeks through the mail.

In retrospect, we probably would not have had to stay in the Army any longer than we did, because the Pacific Theater closed down shortly after the European, and our accumulated points would have gotten us out just as quickly as officers or enlisted men. But we had to make a quick decision and we did it as best we could. It was, as they say, the way the cookie crumbles.

Our front was so static that at one point we were actually playing softball games! Then one day came the sad news—President Roosevelt had died. He was our commander-in-chief, much loved and respected by almost everybody (Rohr had his doubts) and he had just begun his unprecedented fourth term in office. He had been at the helm since the depths of the Depression, had restored our hope in each other and the possibilities of the economy, and had recognized the dangers of the German-Italian-Japanese Axis. He had slowly and deftly (some said much too slowly) brought the United States into the war and determined that our strategy was to defeat Germany first and then Japan. This was not an easy decision because we had been attacked by Japan, not Germany, and there were many who felt happy with the prospect of Germany and Russia going at each other while we concentrated in the Pacific.

All in all, it was considered a great and sobering loss, felt by soldiers and civilians alike. The war in Europe was rushing toward its conclusion and it was a shame that Roosevelt, an architect of the Allied effort, would not be around for the end.

Then, once again, we were ordered to mobilize for what would be our final effort in the war. We packed up in a hurry and then we were on the move. The XVIIIth Airborne Corps had been assigned to the British Second Army (again!) to help in its drive toward the northern part of Germany and the Danish border. We moved off to Munchen-Gladbach and then Braunschweig (both in Germany) moving by motor transport, and then were directed to assemble at the Elbe River at a town named Bleckede, force a river crossing there, and proceed into Germany north of Berlin. Simple as that!

There was almost a holiday atmosphere to this advance as we knew this would be the last campaign. At this point (we were near Braunschweig) Norton called me over and said, "Get ready, we are going to go ahead by plane." One more gulp! What was going on was that Gavin was impatient to get ahead to reconnoiter at Bleckede, he was going to use Major Thornton and his six-seater plane, and that he, Norton, Gavin's bodyguard and I would be the passengers. (This again is one of those adventures that is received with great disbelief by many. However, this is how it happened.)

So I grabbed my rifle and musette-bag and loaded in the rear of the plane along with Norton, Gavin's bodyguard and Sgt. Palmer (the crew chief). Gavin sat up front alongside Thornton. It wasn't a long trip and at the end we were circling around as Thornton located Bleckede and sought a field in which he could land the plane. We could see the Elbe, broad and wandering, below us. There was no sign of military activity. There seemed to be a discussion of where to land and finally Gavin pointed and impatiently said, "There! There!"

Thornton seemed to be following the order reluctantly and shouted back for us to hold on tight while he circled and looked over what seemed to be a tiny field that had been pointed out by Gavin. The field was encircled by trees and appeared to be plowed or planted with a low growing crop (it was the end of April or beginning of May). Thornton brought the plane in, skimming the bordering trees, and touched down with a series of bumps while raising a huge cloud of dust. The plane lurched from side to side—we were hanging on with our hearts in our mouths—as Thornton applied the brakes. It finally stopped with the tail rising slightly, then settling down, and it had stopped almost at the point where we would have wound up in the trees. Some landing! It was hard to resist letting out a cheer.

Anyway, Gavin was out of the plane and all business. He had sighted the area along the river where the crossing was to be made and also a small cluster of buildings that would serve as the staging area for boats which were following by road convoy. We were ready to go on foot. But first we had to help Thornton turn the plane around for a take-off, which would reverse the landing, and promised to be even more tricky. This was done and then Thornton and Palmer grimly got the engine going at full blast, released the brakes and slowly started down the bumpy field. Gaining acceleration, the plane lifted off just when it seemed it was fated to crash, and narrowly made it over the trees. Thornton circled the field and waved a good-bye to us before he flew away.

I had been around Gavin a long time, but never on the ground with him while he was on the march. So off he went with his ground eating strides with Norton at his side and me and the bodyguard bringing up the rear a step behind (as protocol required). He had sighted his route from the air, memorized it, and knew exactly which way to go. How he knew there would be no Germans there is another matter, but there weren't any. After a brief march we were at the cluster of buildings sighted from the air with the glistening Elbe (the Elbe, not the Rhine!) not too far away.

We pushed the door in carefully to what was a deserted tavern, and Gavin and Norton decided this would be our CP. Meanwhile, there were convoys on the road not too far behind us and in a couple of hours some of our first formations arrived. Being there first gave Norton the ability to verbally instruct the arrivals where to assemble. As soon as our follow-up G-3 group arrived, we busied ourselves with assembling and posting a map, putting out the hurried field instructions, and preparing for the coming crossing of the river which would initially be done by small boats using the 82d Reconnaissance Platoon. When the other side was secured, Engineers would build a Bailey Bridge for following groups.

We had been there for half a day and our CP was set up nicely with "my" map board in operation on a raised area on one side of the room (probably normally used by musicians in this tavern). A slight commotion stirred outside the building announcing the arrival of an important visitor and it was the Corps commander, Ridgway, now a Lieutenant General, "visiting the forward troops." He walked in with his flashing eyes taking in the scene, and immediately came over to me and my map and said, "How are you, Sgt. Lebenson?" This may not seem like much so many years later, but believe me, it made my day.

"Very well, Sir," I said. Then it was back to business. There was some German resistance on the other side of the river but not much. The river, however, had been mined, which turned out not to be a problem for the canvas boats. The hastily put-together attack proceeded as planned, and on or about the 1st or 2nd of May we were across the Elbe River, deep into Germany and on a north–south line parallel to Berlin. Only a week or so earlier we had been facing the Rhine. The collapse of Germany was complete, with the Allies closing in from the west and the Russians having been on the outskirts of Berlin for weeks.

After the construction of the Bailey Bridge, our troops poured across the river. There was only a little resistance and very few casualties. The object now was to link up with the Russians who were headed in our direction from the east. Some consideration began to center on the reality of an impending meeting with our ally, and the necessity to make proper recognition and avoid an encounter based on mistaken identity.

Once more we took to the road, this time in a jeep with Norton, with Cooke driving. We were headed for the town of Ludwigslust, which was the site of the palace of the Duke of Mecklenburg and also the area's principal town. It was about at that spot it seemed we would meet the Russians, based on our and their estimated rates of advance.

It was eerie. We had started the war in Sicily with rapid road marches by jeep, and we couldn't help thinking it was Sicily all over again. Also we were obviously elated, felt in a conquering mode, and joyously rode on by ourselves in the heart of Germany, oblivious to danger while seeking the way to Ludwigslust. We felt we were on top of the world. We rounded bend after bend in the road and then, after one turn, there loomed in front of us what seemed to be the whole German Army. They were stretched out along the roadside in disorganized groups, weary, ragged, dispirited and beaten.

But, as we noted quickly, they were still carrying their weapons, even though their means of transport was a jumbled assortment of broken down trucks, tracked vehicles, bicycles, and horse drawn (!) carts. Norton sized up the situation quickly, advised Cooke and I to look as if we really expected all this, and we kept going.

What was happening was that the German Army was broken and defeated and was rushing away from the pursuing Russians, who with good reason they feared, and were hoping to find their way into our hands. Once they saw that they had made it, they just collapsed along the roadside, their esprit and discipline gone, waiting for the next step.

Well, we tried the appearance of conquerors bit and luckily found the town of Ludwigslust still in one piece (us, that is) and parked the jeep outside the Palace and strode in, reconnoitering the place. It was something out of Graustark, with room after room adorned with oil paintings and the halls full of mounted deer heads and horns. There were also rooms filled with filing cabinets, desks, chairs and office machinery. We discovered that the palace had been used as the headquarters of the German Coal Industry and when the British found this

out (remember we were under their ultimate command for this operation), they made plans to remove all the records before the Russians
took over.

There was lots of bustling about and it developed that the
Germans were requesting to surrender on our local front and, as it
developed, it was an entire Army Group that was offering to give itself
in. All this had to be cleared with higher headquarters (not so easy
when dealing with the British), and arrangements were made for the
surrender to be made, that night, in the palace. A document was hastily drawn up, typed, and a German delegation arrived, led by a General
von Tippelskirch in a long leather coat, followed by a bunch of other
officers also in long leather coats. We were using a couple of rooms on
the second floor of the palace. The negotiations were going on in one
room and then Colonel Ireland came into the next room where I was
with some other men, seeking a fountain pen. Well, you guessed it, my
Parker was used for the document, and I had to follow Ireland around
for a while after the event to get it back. (I've since lost it.)

Back to the story. We had won the war—at least in our sector. The
final surrender by Germany to the Allies was still a couple of days off,
but it was over for us. Jimmy had used his bottle of Scotch in the
Gellhorn episode, but I had been saving a bottle of Mumm's Cordon
Rouge Champagne for this occasion. I dug it out of the equipment box
where I'd kept it hidden, pulled Spotswood aside and we went over to
a nearby house on the palace square in which we had thrown our
belongings. There we opened this warm bottle of champagne with a
loud pop, it spilling all over, and we solemnly drank it down in private
celebration.

The excitement was all over. The Germans kept surrendering and
it was so unprecedented that no one knew quite what to do but keep
waving them on. One thing, however, was established: all their
weapons had to be abandoned before crossing a certain point, which
was outside of Ludwigslust. There was an airfield outside of town and
the decision was made that all weapons and ammunition would be
gathered there.

I took advantage of the confusion and, with the Colonel's permission, took off with Cooke in a jeep—our destination being the
German columns before they gave up their weapons with the purpose

of collecting souvenir sidearms for ourselves. (This all sounds crazy now but it's what we did.) We drove out toward the advancing Russians and, in a small hamlet that had a tavern in it, we stopped the jeep and as the Germans passed by, we went over to the officers, many of them on horseback, and, in sign language, asked for their pistols and automatics. Without exception they complied, and in a short time we each had a small bag full. I noticed Cooke had his eyes on watches and I had to tell him that was a no-no, mainly because I could see some danger in collecting something beyond weapons (which were fair game). Also, such a request might be resented and refused. After all, we were in the middle of a German Army, the two of us, and they were fully armed!

We made our way back triumphantly to Ludwigslust, having been gone only a couple of hours and it was still morning. I shared my bounty with a number of the men and gave a P-38 Walther to Colonel Norton. I still kept about a half dozen for myself, including a gorgeous ivory-handled Luger and a small .25 caliber automatic. It was a good haul. Later I traded one of the automatics for a camera and came home with the rest, giving them all away except for a Luger (more about that later).

The day was only starting. Our patrols had met the Russians not too far out of Ludwigslust, and the headquarters of the Red Army facing us was in the town of Grabow, a few miles away. One of our G-3 officers, Captain Novak, had a Slavic background and he understood a little Russian. We also had a Russian interpreter assigned to us from the British Army who was a Russian emigre with a tongue-twister name, which we solved by calling him Snips-snap. Well, Novak was instructed to go over to Grabow with Snips to establish an agreeable demarcation line between us and the Russians and to mark all this up on a map. That's where I came in. So the three of us loaded into Cooke's jeep, with him as driver, and off we headed for Grabow. I was delighted with this assignment because I was anxious to see the Russians firsthand to see if they were as "rough" as we were led to believe.

Approaching the town, as we were recognized, an irregular squadron of horsemen came galloping out to greet us, firing their rifles in the air while whooping it up and uproariously escorting us into town. What a reception! We were hugged and kissed and we could see right away that we would have to be careful or we would all soon be drunk. We wound up in a small house where, after a short while, a groaning table was laid out for us with fruits, vegetables, bread and cold meat and cheese. And vodka! This was a problem because they could easily drink us under the table. Novak handled the situation quite well—we escaped with having to take only a few drinks, exchanged cigarettes (theirs were horrible), marked up the maps, exchanged a lot more hugs and kisses, and were ready to go. Cooke was nowhere to be found. He had not joined us in the meeting but had been toasted into oblivion on the outside. We found him crumpled up on the side of the road and loaded him back into the jeep, while I took over the driving.

We then noticed that there were some fires in buildings in the town. The Russians, more than we, had hatred for the Germans because of the destruction meted to their homeland by the Wehrmacht. The destruction was on the human side as well as on material things. In many respects they had been treated as less than equals by the self-named master race. They were starting to take their vengeance, which would run its course for a while. We could see why the Germans were fleeing them. Our sympathies were clearly with the Russians.

Back to Ludwigslust. One of the reports making the rounds was that there was a slave labor camp not too far away at Wobbelin. Naturally, I had to go there, not as a voyeur but because I wanted to see the Nazis at their worst, always bearing in mind that, but for the grace of God, as a Jew, I and my loved ones could have been there. I never found out how many relatives—cousins, uncles and aunts there were on both sides of my family (as well as my in-laws) who were destroyed by the Germans, but there had to be many.

The next morning I rounded up a couple of guys, got permission from Norton, and drove out to this camp. I was sobered but not sur-prised by everything I saw that morning. What we had been hearing was true. There was a large room stacked with human bodies like sticks of wood. Each body was pitifully skin and bones with the faces frozen into pained grotesque masks. There were also living skeletons there as well, breathing doubles of what we had seen piled up in the room of corpses. Some were lying about on fragments of straw, their ragged garments pulled around their bodies for warmth. They could not understand, or so it seemed, that they were free. We tried to communicate that we were Americans. Some seemed to understand that, most did not. Others were too weak to accept the bits of chocolate I offered from the D-Rations I carried for the occasion. Lifeless men seized upon the cigarettes I offered but then fell away, dizzy from the first puffs.

As quickly as possible we had our medical detachments there to offer what assistance we could. A major problem was food, particularly the kind of food these shadows needed, which was the kind we did not have. We offered water and simple food, then some coffee and cigarettes. Many died in the first days—they were too far gone to be saved. It was a bitter cap to our victory.

Throughout his command, Eisenhower directed that wherever there was a camp in Germany the townspeople would participate in giving a decent burial to those who were found dead in the camps. General Gavin directed that all the men of the town report to the palace grounds and there, in front of the palace in a park-like area, graves were dug by these men in which to lay the bodies brought in from Wobbelin. Before the graves were closed, the German officers from the surrendered Army led a procession that included the entire population of Ludgwigslust at a slow pace around the graves. All were forced to look at the harvest of Hitlerism. Then there was an impressive funeral ceremony and the townspeople closed up the graves. It was a sad ending.

22

HOME

The sobering and sad sequel to the war's ending somewhat tempered the joys of victory. But we had done it! The contribution the 82d had made was second to none—we had served from Africa, through Sicily and Italy and then to England to train for the Big One, followed by the landings in Normandy, subsequent operations in Holland and then the cauldron of Belgium and the Bulge, followed swiftly by the disintegration of the Germans and the campaigns around Cologne and, finally, Ludwigslust in eastern Germany. In circumstances that would change boys into men in a week's time we had been in front-line contact with the enemy for more than 300 sometimes endless days.

Our ranks had been decimated—fortunately it always seemed there were new men to step in and replace the losses. For reasons that make us seem callous and are difficult to fathom, not too much time was spent reflecting on our casualties. At the end we were victorious and essentially felt the flush that comes with victory, the end of danger and of our military careers—and visions of home.

Not only had the Division and its sub-organizations given a good account but we, as individuals, mostly felt that we had contributed. There were, to be sure, the chronic gripers like Jack Rohr and the miserable so-and-so's like Durwood Rusk, but mainly we felt good about ourselves and content in the victory. In the rifle companies, however, where the losses were huge, this feeling was offset by memories of the missing—those that did not make it to the end.

We gathered ourselves together. We knew we were leaving Ludwigslust soon; it was clearly in the Russian zone that had been decided upon many months earlier. There was a lot of bustling about the rooms containing the files and records of the Coal Industry. Shortly before we left the town to the Russians, the British backed in a squadron of trucks and loaded all the files and sped away with them to their zone.

The arms dump at the airfield soon became a mecca for all and sundry, containing, as it did, a massive jumble of weapons and ammunition from the remnants of the 150,000-man Army Group which had surrendered to the 82d. Our war-wise troopers, who had become expert in all forms of weapons, went to collect souvenirs—sidearms, grenades, panzerfausts (German bazookas), flares, rifles and even machine guns. The most fun could be derived from the flares, which could be fired from a large-barreled handgun, and made a great whistling noise and an equally satisfying parabola through the sky. Then the inevitable happened. Something caught and the whole dump erupted in a series of pyrotechnic explosions that alternately flared up and died down over the course of a few days. There was no way the conflagration could be controlled so it was left to run its course. During this period, the noise was similar to some of the sounds of the battlefield, including the intimidating whistling of shells seemingly overhead. I made sure during those couple of days to keep a wall between me and the direction of the airport, just in case.

When the dump finished burning, a few of us went over to the airfield because it had been reported that there was a large number of jet fighters parked there in some hangars. Jets had been used against us first in Holland and, until identified for what they were, caused a great deal of unease. They were unable to be seen because when we looked to where our ear told us the sound was coming from they were long gone, being so much faster than the propeller driven planes we were used to spotting. Their speed afforded them freedom of the skies for a while until the Air Force was able to develop some tactics to use against them. Most fortunate for us, they were in short supply and the Germans didn't have adequate fuel or crews for them. We were impressed with the sight of the propeller-less planes; they looked like they could really fly.

We had set up in the palace but most of it was closed off for protection of the paintings and furniture, etc. In retrospect that probably

was a wise decision, otherwise it would have been damaged and loot-
ed. There seemed to be a fairly rigid policy against looting. I, however, latched onto a good little portable typewriter, which I brought with
me back to France.

Now that the war was over, it opened the way for me to write
some more detailed letters than I was able to earlier. I wrote a long one
about meeting the Russians, also a letter in which I tried to summarize
the places we had been since leaving the States in April of 1943. My
thoughts increasingly turned to coming home. The point system was
going to go into effect and I knew (always subject to some foul-up)
that I had enough so that I wouldn't be part of any movement to the
Far East. Rumors abounded, and since they were not operational matters, I was almost as much in the dark as others, except for what I
could gain from my contact with Charlie Mason in G-1. Everything
was evolving.

We had our little amusements. There was a stable of horses as part
of the palace complex, and Major McCallum, our Provost Marshal,
who was a very big man, each evening tried to ride this particularly
handsome but unruly horse who wouldn't bow to his will. We were all
on the side of the sweat-drenched horse. One day, Hidalgo, who with
the rest of us had idly observed this daily routine, said "Watch me,"
and proceeded to the horse, threw a rope halter over his head, whis-
pered a few gentle Spanish words to him, vaulted onto his back with
no saddle and rode off triumphantly. He had been raised on a ranch
in Del Rio, Texas, and showed that he had been, as he said, born in
the saddle. We congratulated him warmly.

We were going through the motions of organizing training schedules and the like, and we still maintained the up and down reporting
between Division and Corps and Division and Regiment. This kept us
seemingly busy but a lot of it was necessarily make-work, recognized
by all for what it was.

In the meantime there was a series of meetings, including one with
Generals Ridgway and Dempsey and their opposite numbers among
the Russians who now bordered us along a line of many miles length.
There were a lot of hard-drinking sessions among the leaders of both
forces, including one in which one of our battalion commanders
cracked an ankle while demonstrating our jump technique from a sec-

ond story window of the palace. We had the opportunity to mix with the Russians and British, which was good fun and I have a few excellent photos of those meetings. The British had received written instructions as to how they were to "mix" with Russians, basically taking the form of maintaining some form of standoffish British superiority. We found this amusing, to say the least.

A parachute demonstration was laid on at the nearby airport and Dan Bost, our thousand-jump man, did a free fall from several thousand feet and delayed opening his parachute until almost at the point of no return, the chute opening only a short distance above the ground before a heart-pounding audience of Russians. Bost was seized and kissed on both cheeks and decorated on the spot by the senior Russian general.

While in Ludwigslust, a first installment of high-point men was selected for home and discharge, to leave either at the end of May or early June. These men had been around since the early days of the war, had seen all the campaigns and were, mostly, heavily decorated. We followed these developments avidly.

Then, about the end of May, we packed up (not tearfully) and said goodbye to the Russian Zone and Germany, heading first for France and then, hopefully, home! Those of us who harbored bitterness toward the Germans, as did I, were happy to leave the zone to the Russians, because we knew that they would bring some misery to the lives of Germans, as the Russians were not about to give either civilians or soldiers an easy road back. We knew it, the Russians knew it and, above all, the Germans knew it.

Somehow, I happily wound up in a jeep with Major Lekson and we made our way back to Sissonne on our own, buzzing along the autobahn heading for the Dutch border. We had made that visit together earlier to the First Division during the Battle of the Bulge and here we were again, on top of our game, light-hearted in victory as we rolled across Germany, feeling just marvelous. Our plan was to stay over in Nijmegen. I wanted to visit with the van Hoorns, and Lekson had someone he wanted to see in town. We passed the wreckage of Hamburg, one of the most severely damaged German cities, and made it to Nijmegen in a day. We checked into a Canadian installation there, had something to eat and then I found my way down to the van

Hoorns, parked my jeep in their backyard and was welcomed with open arms. The weight of the world was off their shoulders—they had suffered greatly while the war swirled around them for five months after we left in November of 1944—but now they were all smiles, the children healthy and growing, and Alf settled back into his bookstore business. Chrystal continued with her artwork. They were a fine family and we reminisced about the days in September and October when the battle for Nijmegen flowed about them. The next day, I met Lekson at breakfast with the Canadians and then we were on the road, reaching Sissonne without incident.

Our days with the 82d were numbered and we couldn't wait. While going home was our dream, there was a little bittersweetness in leaving what had been home for almost three years. Things actually developed fairly quickly, although it seemed like forever. The demobilization of our armed forces started immediately after VE Day, then accelerated rapidly after victory in Japan, which came only three months later. Then, in another of those moves that are hard to explain, we moved as a body to Epinal, France, concurrent with the Airborne demobilization plan being announced.

The high-point men from all the Airborne Divisions would be transferred into the 17th Division, and the 17th would return to the States and the men would be discharged. The medium-point men would wind up in the 82d, which was now slated for occupational duty in Berlin. The low-point men would then be collected in the 101st for return to the States and would go to the Pacific as might be needed. While this was developing there was still another group of high-point men selected and sent home for discharge. The program they were leaving on was called the Purple Project, which was make-work at its best. In short it used the existing transport aircraft, whose duties were now diminished, by setting up an air route that proceeded across Africa and the South Atlantic to Brazil, then north to the States. The prospect had us all salivating. Home and "making civilian" were coming closer.

In the meantime, our days at Epinal dragged on. There was a French Bastille Day Parade in which we participated, a celebration that broke the monotony. For this event, I deserted my long string of not standing for parades or reviews and joined the rest of the guys marching. We passed through a fairly crowded route in Epinal to cheers and applause. It was exciting.

Shortly after the parade the high-point men were on the way to the 17th. Edison from G-3 and I were on the list, as were Jim Spotswood and Charlie Sippel from G-4. All together there were about ten men and a nucleus of officers from Headquarters. The 82d then would be joined by a large contingent from the 17th and go on to Berlin. We wished them well as we anticipated our good fortune. In leaving the 82d we were really leaving our Army careers and we knew it. I spoke with Colonel Norton and told him how much I had appreciated working with him. Jimmy and I then talked it over and we decided on a move that we would take together and I would like to reserve for the end of this memoir.

Joining the 17th was a comedown, since we felt we were coming from "the" Airborne division to what we considered to be somewhat of a poor relation. We had to change our 82d shoulder patches from one shoulder to the other and sew the 17th Eagle Talon patch onto the left shoulder. We promptly dubbed the Talon patch the "shit hook," which of course endeared us to old 17th hands. We introduced ourselves around; the G-3 was Colonel Messenger, who I had very little to do with in the few weeks I was there.

One of the apparent problems was all the captured weapons that we were carrying. After a few incidents featuring drunken troopers waving loaded revolvers and automatics around, it was quite properly decided by the nervous powers that be to keep all these weapons under guarded lock and key. A notice was posted and a time set for the delivery of all our trophy weapons to a secure area where receipts would be issued and the weapons returned to their owners at the proper time. Many of the men didn't trust this proposal and hung onto their weapons. I turned mine in, including the beautiful Luger. Actually this was a lot safer, I felt, than leaving them in my barracks bag, which was not guarded at all.

As it turned out, the safe haven was broken into and a selective robbery of all the Lugers took place. The other weapons were untouched. Consternation! The reaction to the robbery was a surprise showdown inspection which disclosed all the weapons which had been kept from the original round-up. All these weapons were confiscated, including a number of Lugers. Then a lottery was held among those whose Lugers had been stolen in the break-in. Guess who picked Number One? Me, so I had the choice of the Lugers and I took the best looking one, even though it was far short of the ivory handled beauty I had lost.

The next event was a trip to paradise—a ten-day furlough to Nice on the French Riviera. My roommate and companion on the trip was Charlie Sippel from G-4. Charlie was a soft-spoken, good looking guy from Ohio. It was a pleasure to be with him. We were billeted in a small hotel near the Nice railroad station, but had our meals in the Negresco Hotel, which was one of the luxe hotels on the Promenade des Anglais. The Red Cross had taken over the gambling casino, and served all the things we had grown to crave—Coca-Cola, doughnuts and coffee. We spent our mornings having brandy in a café near our hotel, on the beach in the afternoon and at a café on the Promenade in the evening. It was a heavenly release from the residual tensions of the war. The weather and scenery were miraculous and I knew I would have to come back here some time with Alice (but who knew when). This was the only time in the service when I drank a lot, Sippel and I spending many pleasant hours in bars.

When I returned to Vittel and the 17th Airborne, it was nighttime and there was a note on my cot from Edison. I was on the list of those who were to leave on the Purple Project the next day! Wow! I found out that Jimmy was also on the list and our parallel careers continued. I threw all my stuff together, gathered my weapons from the safe haven the next morning, and was on my way. I hurriedly wrote a letter to Alice, telling her I was leaving, that I didn't know when I would arrive in the States, and also did not know what opportunities I would have to write on the way home.

Our first stop was Thionville, which had been a replacement depot near Luxembourg and was now being used as a station in this reverse movement back to the States. Naturally, as soon as we got there we were advised we would be there for awhile. This was supposed to be flying home to get there in a hurry. Haha. After some time, I got a message to Colonel Gerard (he who as a Captain had given me a Letter of Recommendation for OCS back in Ireland) and was among the officers in our contingent. He came looking for me in the barracks (it wasn't usual for a colonel to be calling on a sergeant) thus enhancing my reputation as someone good to know. Gerard wasn't able to shed any light on our predicament but promised to keep me posted.

To relieve the boredom, I suggested that the First Three Graders (staff sergeant and higher) serve as KP's for a meal, serving the privates, corporals, etc. It was accepted by the other non-coms in good spirit. Another continuing diversion was baiting a non-com who was attached to the replacement depot whose function was to relay orders to us and whose life was made miserable by naming him and calling him "flat-top" after a character in the Dick Tracy comic strip, and also intimidating him by just staring at him. If this was our fun, it was representative of our boredom.

Our squad, which I led as ranking non-com, included Paul Nunan from the 505th, whose broken nose earned him the name "needle-nose" and who wore a DSC and a couple of Silver Stars. Also there was a group of three from the 504th including a platoon sergeant and two of his men. I can only remember the name of one—a private from Florida named Van Paris. These guys passed the time of day by taking turns allowing each other to get a good grip and then fighting his way out. They really got physical. Luckily, they appreciated my exalted position and left me out of those hijinks.

Each day there was a mimeographed sheet of news on a bulletin board, and Jimmy (who headed another squad) and I would mosey over to read it. That's when we saw the report of the atom bomb exploding over Japan. We couldn't digest the description of the power of the bomb, and in addition to not being able to comprehend it didn't really believe it. It gave us a feeling of futility, sort of like we'd had to fight with popguns when super weapons were available. It made what we did look like small potatoes indeed.

And then we were finally off. First by train to Marseilles in southern France, where we encamped for one night. This evening was highlighted after chow with American beer being served on a hillside after being cooled in garbage cans full of cracked ice. The impact of giving each man three whole cans was monumental. I could only drink two, giving the third away. The hillside became full of drunks. Our army in the Pacific served beer on occasion, the British Army rationed it regularly, but for us in the European Theater this was the first time we had seen American spirits since leaving home, and ice cold at that.

Then on to Casablanca in North Africa, where we had started our *Hejira* in April of '43, two years earlier. There we were sorted into planeloads and in a couple of days we were off on a journey which took us in stages to Dakar (West Africa), over the ocean to Belem in Brazil, then on to Georgetown in British Guiana, to Puerto Rico and, finally, Miami, where we all left the plane and joyously kissed the ground. In Dakar we had an event similar to the beer in Marseilles. A canned chocolate drink called "Sambo" was iced and offered to us in the can. It was the sweetest thing we'd had in years and actually made some of the men sick from its richness.

At each of these stops there was the usual showdown inspection and the admonition against carrying money (which we all disregarded). One of the men, Dolan, came from the gas house section of New York City and he was carrying a German light machine gun with him which, naturally, he could not hide. He also had a box of ammunition along with it. He was dogged in his determination to keep it even though we all told him it would be taken away. At each showdown we thought this would be the one but he held onto it through all those inspections and arrived in the United States still carrying it. It became a continuing joke, which only ended with him striding out of Pennsylvania Station in New York, now a civilian, onto Seventh Avenue with the machine gun over his shoulder.

Things had become a blur. From Miami we were taken by train to Camp Blanding in northern Florida, being cheered on by crowds which some committee or other gathered at railroad stations along the way. I had been able to get a phone call home to an equally excited Alice and it was not going to be too much longer, although there were still stops along the way.

At Blanding, women volunteers sewed on insignia for us and we shed our 17th patches and had our proud 82d ones placed back where they belonged. After Blanding, we headed for discharge centers across the country and were therefore divided by area. Our group was headed for Fort Dix in New Jersey. Then things moved rather swiftly. The discharge process took a day or so, during which time all of us turned down the "opportunity" to stay in the Army Reserve (the inducement being holding onto rank).

And then the joyful/nervous train ride to New York. Nunan was with me—he lived in Syracuse and for some reason seemed to have great trepidation about going home. He didn't want to head there immediately and I suggested he stay in a hotel overnight. I dropped him off from a taxi at the Hotel Lexington and I continued over the bridge to Long Island City, a Ulysses returning to be greeted by wife and family, ready to pick up the pieces and begin all over again. My nephew, Roaul, saw me getting out of the cab and ran up the stairs to Alice's apartment, alerting everybody before I had paid off the driver. I burst into the apartment to greet and be greeted by Alice with a mighty hug, and then finally had my first sight of my son. Home at last!

But this tale should end with what was essentially the final act of my career in the Army. Before leaving the 82d, Spotswood and I talked it over and decided we would make a formal good-bye, requesting a brief meeting with General Gavin through his aide, Captain Thompson. We stood in front of the General, caps in hand after having saluted, and one of us spoke: "We are leaving today for the 17th. Before we do, we decided we could not go without telling you what an honor it has been for both of us to have served with the 82d, particularly under your command."

Gavin had become a legendary figure to all paratroopers and was held in deep affection. He was young, handsome and athletic. Above all, he was fearless. He accepted our comments gracefully, told us in turn how valuable we had been and wished us well. He extended his hand to us; we shook, then drew up to attention, saluted, turned on our heels and left the office.

Ahead of us was resumption of life at home with our families, which we had eagerly dreamed of for nearly three years. Our military careers had ended.

AFTERWORD

Well, I did it and, as they say, I'm glad.

I find I wish I had written this earlier while many of the details were clearer. There may be several mistakes in time, place and personnel, none of them intentional. I wish I had been able to recall details that would have brought some of my comrades in arms more into focus, since I was privileged to serve with an exceptional group of men.

I'm also glad this is on paper for my wife and children and the future generations of my family.

But also one of the reasons for writing has been the obvious disbelief some ex-soldiers (with whom I did not directly serve) have had with some of my experiences. Though my role in the war was not of my own creation or choosing, those experiences do make my history a little unique, as they include:

- Direct assignment to the 82d Airborne from Induction Center. Immediate pigeon-holing for assignment to G-3.
- Selection by Hq & HQ Co as advance man to the Washington.
- Freedom of the ship during the Atlantic Crossing.
- Selection as one of two enlisted men to accompany General Ridgway on the command ship going into Sicily.
- Observing Patton from close up on the *Monrovia*.
- Climbing down that rope ladder for a D-Day landing in Sicily.
- Being present when Ridgway briefed his commanders on Giant, the projected occupation of Rome.

211

- Return to Sicily from Naples as part of the pathfinding project.
- Designation as the person to pick up ship's manifests as the rear echelon left Sicily.
- Selection as one of two men to accompany Colonel Rusk from Ireland to be briefed on proposed Division billeting in England.
- Bigoted status for Normandy (also other campaigns as well).
- Attendance at Exercise Dart two weeks before D-Day—final rehearsal for Overlord, Montgomery in charge.
- Selection as the one man in G-3 to go in with the initial assault in Normandy.
- D-Day in Normandy.
- Parachute school in England.
- D-Day in Holland.
- Trip on my own back to England to get After Action Report printed.
- Dash to Belgium—first jeep on the road after movement orders were published.
- Flight to Bleckede near end of war in an advance group of four, including General Gavin.
- Return home by Purple Project.

All the above happened. Jim Spotswood of G-2 had a similar career. Along the way there were a lot of incidents and characters, some of them mentioned in this memoir. There was a real villain in Colonel Rusk—all the men despised him. There were some great officers as well; in my case Colonels Weinecke and Norton, who both did a lot for me. Oddly enough, about forty-five years after the war, at a Division reunion, I was having breakfast with Norton and Tallerday (who had been S-3 of the 505th) and Rusk's name came up and Norton observed, "Rusk? He was a fine officer." That's the only thing I hold against Jack Norton.

I believe I served well. The big disappointment was not going to Officer's Candidate School. Maybe that was for the better. I might have wound up as an infantry platoon leader, the category that had the greatest casualty rate in the service. As it played out, I found my niche and was fortunate in being truly surrounded by heroes—the officers and men of the 82d Airborne Division.

A lot has been written about World War II. The books authored by Stephen Ambrose and Tom Brokaw have brought our exploits into sharp focus. What my effort might do is add some insight into the functions of a headquarters during combat—from an enlisted man's point of view.

My thanks to all who have taken the time to read these pages.

June 2007

29 Mar 85.

Dear Lebenson,

I am deeply appreciative of your gracious letter.

Coming from one with whom I was privileged to share combat service in our magnificent 82 d Airborne Division, it could not mean more.

Providence was good to us both and we were fortunate to have such a privileged opportunity to serve.

With every good wish, and with warm thanks,

Sincerely

M. B. Ridgway
General, U.S. Army
Retired.

Mr. Leonard Lebenson

44 Summit Road

Elizabeth, New Jersey.

07208.

Forty years later. A letter from General Matthew Ridgway, one of the author's prized possessions.